HomeGrown Faith

*You Can Nurture Your Kids
in the Christian Faith!*

David

and

Kathy

Lynn

world
PUBLISHING
SINCE 1926

Printed in the United States of America
1 2 3 4 5 — 09 08 07 06

Amy and Megan
Time spent with you is a gift.

Contents

Section One:
HomeGrown Faith for Every Parent

Section Two:
Fifty Nifty HomeGrown Faith Activities You Can Do
with Your Kids and Grandkids

Acknowledgments

Books are not written in a vacuum. People of all kinds influence their development. *HomeGrown Faith* is no exception. We have had hundreds of people of faith shape who we are and what we think. We would like to thank a few of those people here. Frank Couch at World Publishing believed in what we had to say and for that we are grateful. Ramona Richards, Debbie Evert, and Amanda Haley, our editors, get the credit for making the book a better read. Dick Hardel, David Anderson, Marilyn Sharpe, Lyle Griner, Jim LaDoux, and Dee Seaquist, all at the Youth and Family Institute, have been a powerful inspiration encouraging us to keep on encouraging parents and grandparents to pass on the faith.

A big thank you goes out to Linda Staats of the Grand Canyon Synod of the ELCA for her input into the development of the *Top Ten HomeGrown Faith Practices for Parents* as well as her encouragement. Wayne Rice has always been a mentor and supporter. Thanks Wayne. We are deeply grateful to Jim Burns for his contribution and encouragement. Bill Inboden was a critical faith conversation partner. Thanks for putting up with my (David's) musings about families, congregations, and passing on the Christian faith.

Last, but not least, thanks to Amy and Megan Lynn, our daughters, who have taught us that home can be church too.

Thanks to all of you for helping to make *HomeGrown Faith* possible.

David and Kathy Lynn
Tucson, Arizona

Foreword

Dr. Jim Burns

All reputable studies tell us that the single most important social influence on the spiritual lives of adolescents is their parents. Of course, there are other great mentors like grandparents, youth workers, and peers, but parents have the greatest lasting impact on the spiritual lives of their kids. Dave and Kathy Lynn understand this fact as well as anyone in the world, and *HomeGrown Faith* is the best-researched and most practical book I have ever read on this subject.

A phrase I often repeat to church leaders is this: One of the major responsibilities of the church is to mentor parents; parents then mentor their children; and the legacy of faith continues to the next generation. Frankly, there is no greater biblical calling than for parents to be intentional about energizing their family's spiritual lives.

The Bible is very clear that our job is to pass our faith from generation to generation. At HomeWord (where I work), we have a Web site that receives several million visitors each year. We ask visitors to check the top three parenting issues that interest them most, ranking what they desire for their family from their most important values to their least important values. Every month, the number one issue of interest to parents is that of passing on your faith. Not only is this a biblical mandate, it's our calling.

At the same time, you may be like my wife and I and find yourself saying, "I don't feel qualified to help my children grow spiritually." As Dave and Kathy write in this book, "The only qualification is a willing heart." I don't know about you, but that is very refreshing to me. Now, since you are reading this foreword, I would imagine you have a very willing heart with a desire to see an eternal spiritual legacy happen for your family. Many of us have the desire, but we need the blueprint for a solid *Home-Grown Faith*. With the Scripture as their guide, Dave and Kathy have done just that—given us a blueprint. It's very difficult, if not impossible, to build a home without following a blueprint. Yet many people allow their family to grow spiritually by circumstance and chance.

As you read this outstandingly well-researched and practical book, you will be reminded over and over again that **parents do matter** to their kids! Parents matter when it comes to important issues, faith, school, drug and alcohol use, and a host of other life-transforming issues. Your influence and impact make an eternal difference. You can offer blessings or curses to your kids. Both will often make a lifelong, lasting impression. This book will teach you how to offer blessings.

My suggestion is to use this book in several ways. Read *HomeGrown Faith*. It's practical, it's biblical, it's challenging, and it will give you a blueprint to build a legacy of faith for your family. But don't just *read* the book. After each chapter, there are stimulating questions for reflection and for dialogue. You can talk with your spouse (if you are married), and I would suggest that you discuss the group questions with a small group from your church or neighborhood.

My wife Cathy and I were in a couples' small group for several years during some formative years in the lives of our three daughters. In many ways, the entire group helped us to raise our kids. I strongly encourage you to use this book in a group format.

Finally, don't forget to use some of the "fifty nifty" ideas with your own family. David Lynn is one of the finest youth ministry experiential education experts in getting kids to talk about important subjects. Youth workers have used his material successfully for years. The ideas (beginning on Page 81) are practical, fun, easy-to-do, and inspiring. So get your kids talking about spiritual issues by using some of these great ideas in the book.

Here's a little test. What is the most often quoted scripture in the Bible? John 3:16? Psalm 23? No. It's Deuteronomy 6:4-9. In Hebrew, it's called the *Shema*. It is the holy strategy of the Hebrew people, and in every orthodox Jewish home today, it is quoted most every morning and evening. The Shema is recited at important feasts and holidays. When Jesus was asked, "What is the most important commandment?", He immediately quoted part of Deuteronomy 6. In fact, these words might have been some of the first Scripture that was ever taught to Jesus. Here's what it says:

> *Listen, Israel! The LORD our God is the only true God! So love the LORD your God with all your heart, soul, and strength. Memorize his laws and tell them to your children over and over again. Talk about them all the time, whether you're at home or walking along the road or going to bed at night, or getting up in the morning. Write down copies and tie them to your wrists and foreheads to help you obey them. Write these laws on the door frames of your homes and on your town gates (De 6:4-9).*

That is our calling as parents. Church leaders are called to come alongside parents in our congregations and to follow the words of the Shema. *HomeGrown Faith* will help you follow the blueprint in that calling.

Thanks, Mom

You never think it will happen to your family. I know we didn't.

On a normal Wednesday afternoon in April 2005, I received the phone call that would change our family forever. "David, Mom's dead," my sister said. "She's been shot." I think my brain shut down at that point because I barely remember hearing the details.

My parents lived in a retirement community in Sun City, Arizona. On that day, my mother had been sitting in the audience at a board meeting for their homeowner's association. My father, one of the board members, was sitting on the stage with four other members. The meeting was going on as planned when a man with a gun suddenly burst into the meeting and began firing at the board members. One woman was killed and three others were injured. The man aimed the gun at my father, but the gunman was jumped from behind and the gun jerked down as it fired, hitting my mother. She died in my father's arms.

"What do I do!" I wanted to scream. I didn't want to believe it. I wanted to drive the 150 miles from Tucson to Sun City to make it all better. This wasn't supposed to happen, not to my family! My next thought was in some ways even more frantic: how do I tell my kids that their grandmother had been shot by a psycho?

As my wife and I tried to explain to my girls what happened, I waited for the question. "Why? Why did God let this happen to Nana?" Her random death was at the hands of someone mentally unstable, and I wasn't sure I knew the answer to that God question. We had plenty of time to talk about that and other questions the next day as we drove to Sun City to be with my father and five brothers and sisters. We talked about my mom and her commitment to her faith and how she and my dad nurtured the Christian faith with us at home and in their small congregation. We talked about how all six of Mom's children had grown up to be Christfollowers and marry Christians, and how all 11 grandchildren were growing up as Christians. None of this answered the "Why?" question, but it did help us to see clearly the strong faith influence my mom had.

In Sun City, we embraced our other family members, still relishing the memories of Mom and her great faith but with the same question in our minds. Then we learned that the local and national media had picked up on our story and wanted to do more in-depth coverage. It became very clear that this tragedy could somehow be used for good. The story of a faithful mother of six and her 11 Christ-following grandchildren was featured on the local news, and when our family decided to make a statement of forgiveness to the man who had pulled the trigger, an opportunity came to share the story of God's grace.

As people visited or called with their condolences, we heard stories of how my mom's faith had impacted others outside our family. It seemed that almost everyone we spoke to had been touched by Mom's faith. There were stories of her as a Sunday school teacher, Bible School teacher, and nursery worker. In fact, it seemed that if a program was available at church, she was part of it.

Although I was aware of her involvement in her congregation when I was growing up, what I was more aware of was the influence of her faith at home. She told us Bible stories and sang worship songs with us. She encouraged all of us to read our Bibles and tell others about God's love. She invited our friends—and their families—to Sunday school. She was a force to be reckoned with!

Maybe that is why more than 1,700 people packed the church for her memorial service. With television cameras rolling, they heard my father, her six children, and several of her grandchildren talk about the influence her faith had on our lives and how Jesus' love is there for all. Through her children and grandchildren, her legacy lives on in the people they touch, in turn, as teachers, ministers, musicians, missionaries, and parents of their own children. Who knows how many people were touched during that service. I would never want to live this tragedy over again, but I know God used the situation in a big way.

Thanks, Mom, for the homegrown faith!

Yet I wanted to do more for my mother's legacy than be grateful for the faith she passed on to my children and me. This book is the result. Section One of the book provides you with an overview of the "Whys" of a homegrown faith. Fifty practical ideas are outlined in Section Two. "Parents Matter" sidebars are also included, featuring the research that demonstrates the influence parents have on their children and teenagers. We want you to be thoroughly convinced by the end of the book that you, as a parent, have enormous influence on the formation of faith and values in your kids.

In addition, "Could You Do This?" sidebars give practical faith practices for you to try. Some of these activities have been used in the stories of our three families—the Collins, Davis, and Goodman families. Let me introduce these folks, whom you'll get to know intimately as they grow and develop their own homegrown faith.

Liz and Sam Collins have three kids: Dan, the oldest; Louie; and daughter Carla. Dan grows up to marry Beth and has two kids: Joy and Danny. Louie has a son named Josh.

Bonnie and Frank Davis have three kids: their oldest is son Chris; then there's daughter Jenna and son K.C.

The Goodman family is headed by the matriarch, Anna, who has a son named Joe. He and his wife Sandy have two boys, Matt and Joey. Matt's daughter's name is Leah. She and her husband Jeff are expecting Matt's first grandchild.

So . . . let's join them and get growing!

David and Kathy Lynn
Tucson, Arizona

HomeGrown Faith for Every Parent

Chapter One

The Deuteronomy Promise

Each generation tells the next about your faithfulness (Is 38:19b).

The Davis Family

One Saturday morning Frank stood at the kitchen counter making a pot of coffee. "You ready to go, hon?" he called to his wife.

Bonnie walked into the kitchen, a puzzled look on her face. "Go? Where are we going?"

"Come on, Bonnie." Frank reached for a cup. "We talked about going to look at big screen TVs this morning. I've done a lot of research, and I know the one we should get. There's a sale this weekend, and I want to get to the store before they are all gone."

"I know we talked about it, but I told you that I wanted to spend today at home with the family." Bonnie watched the coffee finish brewing then poured cups for both of them. "We haven't read the Bible together or prayed or even talked together as a family in I don't know how long."

"Don't worry. We'll be with the family," Frank said, "just a little later."

Bonnie sighed. "I know. It's just that when you start shopping, 'a little later' could mean several hours."

Down the hall, Jenna left her bedroom and headed for the kitchen. As she passed her older brother's room, a hand reached out and pulled her back. "Hey," she said to Chris as she wiggled to get out of his grip. "What do you think you're doing? I was just going to the kitchen. I'm hungry."

"Don't go in there now. Mom and Dad are fighting."

"Again! Now what are they fighting about?" Jenna dropped down on the edge of his bed. "It seems like they are always fighting these days."

"I know!" Chris rolled his eyes. "This time it's because Dad wants to go shopping with Mom, and she wants us all to be home together today."

"I remember Mom saying that she wanted to talk with us and pray and stuff," said Jenna. "She doesn't think we do enough together as a family anymore."

The voices from the kitchen grew louder, and Chris and Jenna went to his door to listen.

"Come on, Bonnie! The kids get enough of that stuff at church. You want us to be together? Just think how much fun we can have together with a big screen TV."

"But we need to spend more time with the kids talking about important things."

"Our family is fine!" Frank's voice grew a bit edgier. "Why can't you lighten up a little? I tell you what ... *you* stay here and talk religion with the kids, and I'll go check out the TVs by myself." Leaving his coffee on the counter, Frank left.

After the awkward good-bye, Bonnie stood in the family room and prayed. "Help me, Lord. Help my family grow closer to you. Open Frank's heart to this need. Amen."

When she was finished praying, Bonnie asked the kids to join her in the family room. She could tell by their silence that they had heard the argument. She decided that the time had come to stop waiting for Frank to join them.

"Well," she began as she turned to face the kids. "I suppose you heard your dad and me talking."

"It was kind of hard not to, Mom," Jenna said.

"I know, Sweetie." Bonnie gently touched Jenna's head.

"Are we really getting a big screen TV?" K.C., the youngest, squirmed on the couch.

"It looks that way," Bonnie said. "But that's not what I wanted to talk about. Since we're home together today, I'd like to spend time getting closer to each other and especially to God. We've been neglecting praying together and reading our Bibles. I found an interesting book of Bible devotions that might be fun for us to try today."

The three Davis kids looked at each other. It wasn't exactly how they wanted to spend the day, but their mom looked so hopeful, it would be tough to refuse.

"Sure, Mom." Chris gave her a quick hug. "Show us what you got."

The Collins Family

"Oh, my word!" Liz gasped as she looked at the calendar. She had gotten it out to mark the next time she needed to take cupcakes to her daughter's scout troop meeting. She counted the weeks again.

"What?" Her husband Sam looked up from the sports section of the newspaper.

"Do you realize that it's been over a month since we've been to church?" Liz said. "That can't be right." She re-counted the weeks. "Nope, I'm right, four weeks!"

"Really?" Sam asked. "It doesn't seem that long to me. I thought we just went a couple of weeks ago."

Liz walked over to sit beside her husband at the kitchen table. "We have had something every weekend for the last month. It's either baseball, swimming, or trips to the lake."

"We are kind of busy, aren't we?"

"We probably should go this Sunday. I don't want the kids to think we don't want to go to church anymore," Liz said.

"Can't." Sam bit into a muffin.

"Can't what?"

Sam swallowed. "We can't go this Sunday. Louie has a baseball game, and I'm assistant coach. We can't miss the game."

"Right. How could I forget that?" Liz paused and took a deep breath. "Well, we could do an activity from that new book the pastor was talking about. It's supposed to have a lot of faith activities for families to do together."

"Faith activities?" Sam asked suspiciously. "I'm not sure we know enough to do something like that. What if we mess up the kids?"

"I don't know, but how hard could it be? I looked at the book and all we have to do is read a story and a passage from the Bible and then talk about a few questions."

"It doesn't sound too bad, but I still don't think I'm ready to commit to something like that. Why don't we just keep going to church?"

"OK. What about Sunday night? I've been hearing good things about that worship service. I think the kids would like the worship band they have."

"I don't know, hon," Sam replied. "We always get home so late when we go to church on Sunday nights. I think it gives the week a bad start because we wind up rushing around when we get home, trying to get things ready for the next day. I don't think that's good for the kids."

"I guess you're right. Between homework, laundry, and packing lunches, Sunday night is pretty full. I just worry that the kids aren't learning enough about spiritual things. Oh, well, maybe we can go next Sunday."

"Hmm?" Sam bit off another chunk of his muffin. "Oh, right. Don't worry, Liz, we have plenty of time for that. We'll see what's going on next week, and maybe we can go then."

The Goodman Family

"What are we doing today?" Joey was still a bit confused about his life now that his parents were both working.

"Let's go over it again, honey." His mother gathered a couple of toys and a book off the front seat as she talked. "You'll be staying with Grandma during the day. She's going to take you to church with her, then some place cool for lunch." Sandy paused for a second as she helped her boys get out of the car. "Then Dad will pick you up here and take you home. And I'll see you all tonight when I get off work."

Joey, his brother Matt, and their mom climbed the steps to their grandma's front door.

"I'm glad we're going to church with Grandma," Matt said.

"Good." Sandy rang the doorbell. "What part do you like best?"

"The singing," Joey said.

"She asked me, Joey." Matt scowled at his brother, then looked up at his mom. "I like the singing, too, but what I really like are the Bible stories that Grandma tells on the way back. She tells stories about what the minister was talking about." In a lower voice, he confided, "Sometimes I don't understand the ones the pastor talks about."

"I'm glad you understand Grandma's version," said Sandy.

"There are my sweeties!" called a voice through the opening door. Grandma Anna threw open her arms for a hug.

"Thanks, Mom." Sandy hugged her mother-in-law. "We really appreciate you. The kids are excited about going to church."

"Me too! We'd better get going or we'll be late," Anna said as she helped Matt and Joey carry their things into the house. They followed her in, dropped everything on the couch, then scrambled for her car. After church and lunch, all three of them stretched out for a nap.

When they woke up, Matt asked, "Can we watch TV, Grandma?"

"Not now, Matt," she said. "I have a better idea."

"What?"

"Let's draw pictures of some of our favorite stories in the Bible."

"Will you draw with us, Grandma?" Joey asked.

"Sure," she said.

"What kind of pictures can we draw?" Matt asked.

Anna pulled crayons and pads out of a drawer. "How about Noah's ark or David and Goliath?"

"You mean the giant?" Joey reached for one of the pads.

"I like to draw giants," Matt said.

"What will you draw, Grandma?" Joey peered into the crayons for his favorite color.

"I think I'll draw heaven."

"Will you draw Grandpa in heaven?" Joey asked.

"Yes, Joey," his grandmother replied. "I think I will."

Matt began his version of Goliath with a couple of bold marks across the paper. "This is great Grandma, even better than TV."

Anna smiled.

Catching Faith at Home

You can predict with a certain amount of accuracy where each of these families is headed spiritually. Why? Because the future does not arrive unannounced! Each set of parents is laying the groundwork for whether or not their children will be Christ followers as adults.

Bonnie Davis is headed in the right direction to pass on the faith to her children regardless of what Frank chooses. Her commitment to both congregation and homegrown faith is evident. You sense that, despite her marital problems, Bonnie's kids will be people of faith as adults.

What about the Collins kids, however? What will become of their spiritual lives when Sam and Liz think that faith formation is the job of the church? They attend a congregation when it is convenient and hope that is enough.

Then there is the Goodman family. Despite the tough work schedule Mom and Dad face, they are committed to leaving a legacy of faith, the same type Grandma Anna left for her son. Do you think Jesus will be Lord of the Goodman kids when they are adults?

Faith is caught more than it is taught! Lack of faith is also contagious. The kids in all three families are catching something from home. From Frank Davis, they are catching a sense that faith in Christ is a bother, even as they can see Bonnie living a life that shouts, "Nurturing faith in our lives is worth the effort."

Sam and Liz Collins are passing on the notion that growing in Christ is all right at the church building, sometimes, unless something better comes along. And finally, there's Grandma Anna, who takes seriously her responsibility to pass on the Christian faith to her grandchildren.

Your Kids and the Deuteronomy Promise

Your kids are no different. They will catch something from you as you live out your faith in everyday family life. It takes more than going to a church building to pass on the Christian faith. We would like to think that our children, including our teenagers, can "catch" Jesus in the church building. They can't! They can only encounter Jesus through loving, caring relationships. They can learn *about* Jesus in church—His birth, the miracle of the five loaves and the two fishes, the Sermon on the Mount, His death and resurrection—but to experience the grace that God offers requires personal relationships.

Don't take this wrong. Learning *about* Jesus is critical, and congregations offer many wonderful opportunities for this sort of instruction, such as Sunday school, Vacation Bible School, small group studies, children's church, youth groups, etc. But as wonderful as these opportunities are, they can only *supplement* what is happening at home. They can never *replace* what God can do through you within the normal routines of your family life. No matter how creative the Bible story time is during Sunday school, no matter how many Bible verses are memorized at Vacation Bible School, no matter how many small group studies your children attend—none can replace a homegrown faith.

Being involved with a church is vital, and, yes, the relationships you and your children have with members of your congregation are critical to nurturing faith within your children, including your teenagers. Your fellow believers, however, have a limited influence on faith formation when compared to *you*. The chances of your kids catching faith dramatically increase when faith is expressed, talked about, and lived out within the normal routines of your family life. The home remains the primary influence of faith and values.

Sprinkled throughout this book are the results of research that clearly demonstrate the awesome influence *you* have on your kids. We were inspired to present this research from a quote by Dolores Curran, a family strengths expert. She said, way back in 1980, that "we need to gather together the impressive data showing that the parent is the primary determinant of a person's faith, and present it over and over in every way possible until we convince parents of its validity. Until we do so, parents will continue to visualize themselves as adjuncts to the faith process. Adjuncts do not necessarily become responsible."[1]

Parents have the power to influence the faith of their children. Is that influence a guarantee that your children will follow Jesus as adults? No, but your influence is substantial. More than school teachers, coaches, counselors, Sunday school teachers, pastors, peers, youth workers, mentors, the Internet, or the media, your contribution to the

---

[1] Dolores Curran. "Family Ministry," in *Family Ministry* (Minneapolis, MN: Winston Press, 1980), 17.

faith and values your children will live out in their adult lives is *the most* significant. Kids who follow Christ as adults apart from the influence of their parents are the *exception,* not the rule, and as children they were most likely influenced by other kids whose parents were people of faith. The rule is that your kids will become what you are at home! As you will see, God's plan for passing on faith to your children is portrayed indisputably in Scripture. We call this plan the "Deuteronomy Promise."

The "Deuteronomy Promise"

God's wonderful plan for living by faith is best passed on to children, including teenagers, through the home's normal routines of family life. This way, kids, their parents, and their extended family can together experience the joy of living in grace as they follow Christ. These kids will choose to be Christfollowers as adults (De 6:4-7, 20-25; 11:1-28; 32:46-47).

What Does the Research Say?

We have more than 40 years of social science research that clearly demonstrates parents are the primary influencer of faith and values in children, including teenagers. This reality flies in the face of popular psychology and conventional wisdom that has misled parents and adults into incorrectly thinking that peers are the primary influencer on the lives of children, especially teenagers. **Not true!** Let us examine just one recent study that illustrates what this convincing body of research has to say to parents.

The "National Study of Youth and Religion" was a research project on the religious and spiritual lives of teenagers in the United States. Conducted by the University of North Carolina at Chapel Hill from 2001 to 2005, the study offers concrete evidence of the influence of parents on the faith lives of their children. Read what the authors said as they stated a recurring theme of their research: "The evidence clearly shows that the single most important social influence on the religious and spiritual lives of adolescents is their parents. Grandparents and other relatives, mentors, and youth workers can be very influential as well, but normally, parents are most important in forming their children's religious and spiritual lives. Teenagers do not seem very reflective about or appreciative of this fact. But that does not change the reality that the best social predictor, although not a guarantee, of what the religious and spiritual lives of youth will look like is what the religious and spiritual lives of the parents do look like."[2]

What implications does this study have for you as a parent? First and foremost, know that you have a profound influence on the faith development of your kids, for good or for ill.

Second, your kids—especially as teenagers—will not appreciate your influence. Get over it. They will probably need to have their own children before they understand all that you are doing and will do for them. Don't expect a thank you for the struggling you do to keep God a constant presence within your home. Forget being appreciated for struggling to have mealtime faith conversations. Try not to get too down that your kids do not see the importance of family prayers. Keep on keeping the faith! See the big picture—your kids following Christ as adults. It is worth your efforts.

Finally, remember your kids are watching *you* and how you live out the Christian faith within the normal routines of family life.

> **Could You Do This?**
>
> Bonnie stopped beside Jenna's door. She looked in at her sleeping daughter, then closed her eyes and began to pray. Her husband Frank thought she was being silly, but Bonnie didn't care; her kids needed someone praying for them. It was such a simple thing really. All she did was stand outside the doors of her kids' rooms and take time to talk with God about them. She had already prayed for her boys outside their bedroom, asking God to help heal the finger that K.C. had sprained in gym class and to help Chris as he struggled with the latest math problems. Now it was Jenna's turn.
>
> "Lord, be with my little girl," she prayed. "Keep her safe and help her make good decisions. Amen."
>
> Finishing her prayer, Bonnie took a step toward her own room when she heard a small voice say, "Amen."
>
> Bonnie stopped, and a slow smile spread over her face. Jenna had been listening. "Thank you, Lord," she whispered.

What Does God Say?

Let's take a short walk through the Bible to see what God has to say about passing on the faith to our children. We will begin our walk in the Old Testament Book of Deuteronomy, the fifth book of the Bible. Moses has already led the Israelites out of slavery in Egypt and around the wilderness for 40 years. The people are about to enter the land God promised them. In the sixth chapter of Deuteronomy, Moses outlines God's plan of peace and prosperity for these people.

> The LORD told me to give you these laws and teachings, so you can obey them in the land he is giving you. Soon you will cross the Jordan River and take that land. And if you and your descendants want to live a long time, you must always worship the LORD and obey his laws (De 6:1-2).

---

[2] Christian Smith and Melinda Lundquist Denton. *Soul Searching: The Religious and Spiritual Lives of American Teenagers* (Oxford, England: Oxford University Press, 2003), 261.

Could You Do This?

"Buckle up, guys," Anna said.

"Okay, Grandma." Matt got in the back seat and put on his seat belt.

His brother Joey did the same thing. "What kind of flowers are we getting?"

"I thought we might get some marigolds to plant in the window boxes." Anna paused to turn on the CD player and hum along with the music.

"You must really like that music," Matt said. "You play it all the time."

"I do like it," Anna said. "It's all about how great God is and how much God loves us."

"I bet God likes to listen to it," said Joey.

"You know, Joey, I bet He does, too." Anna said.

This is not the voice of a demanding or condemning God. This is the voice of a God with high expectations for us.

Pay attention, Israel! Our ancestors worshiped the LORD, and he promised to give us this land that is rich with milk and honey. Be careful to obey him, and you will become a successful and powerful nation (De 6:3).

Notice Moses specifically tells the people to "pay attention." We should also listen. God gave those people (and us as well) a promise. Follow God's Plan A, and your lives will be less difficult than if you neglect that plan. Notice we said "less difficult." Life in our fallen world, stained by sin, is difficult. And just because you are a Christian does not mean life is easier. But try to live your life apart from God's plan and, believe it or not, life gets even more difficult. For example, the Ten Commandments are not suggestions. Fail to live by them and life gets ugly. But you know this already. You only need to look at your past to see the consequences you have paid for neglecting God's Plan A. If we are honest with ourselves, we know the results of detours. At best, it is guilt and shame; at worst, it is disaster.

Fortunately, God's grace is available to anyone who asks. God gives us a Plan B and a Plan C and a Plan D and more. His grace is still available. And the promise is always there—live by God's plan and reap the rewards.

After giving God's plan for living, Moses interjects some first-rate theology followed by some practical advice.

Listen, Israel! The LORD our God is the only true God! So love the LORD your God with all your heart, soul, and strength. Memorize his laws (De 6:4-6).

Ask yourself this question: "How would my life be different and better if I consistently believed this theology and lived out this advice?" The obvious answer to this question is, "Much smoother than my life is going now!" Of course, that assumes we are living a life wholly devoted to the triune God of the universe, following all that He asks of us.

Now what? Moses gives the best parenting advice you will ever receive:

And tell them to your children over and over again. Talk about them all the time, whether you're at home or walking along the road or going to bed at night, or getting up in the morning (De 6:7).

Love God! Live God! Talk God with your children! What a great plan for parenting. And remember the promise—we are not passing on the faith through the normal routines of family life just to glorify or honor God, but for the good of our kids as well as ourselves. There are awesome benefits for following Christ, both temporal and eternal.

> *That's why the LORD our God demands that we obey his laws and worship him with fear and trembling. And if we do, he will protect us and help us be successful (De 6:24).*

> *You know that the LORD your God is the only true God. So love him and obey his commands, and he will faithfully keep his agreement with you and your descendants for a thousand generations (De 7:9).*

Let's see how the children of Israel did with God's plan for living an abundant life and passing on faith-filled living to the next generation.

> *Joshua had been faithful to the LORD. And after Joshua sent the Israelites to take the land they had been promised, they remained faithful to the LORD until Joshua died at the age of one hundred ten. He was buried on his land in Timnath-Heres, in the hill country of Ephraim north of Mount Gaash. Even though Joshua was gone, the Israelites were faithful to the LORD during the lifetime of those men who had been leaders with Joshua and who had seen the wonderful things the LORD had done for Israel (Ju 2:6).*

Parents Matter: Faith Practices

A look at the research

What faith practices does research indicate are effective at passing on the faith in families? A study of more than 2,000 adults and young people by the Search Institute found four family practices that nurtured faith in children, including teenagers.

Faith Talk with Mom
Faith Talk with Dad
Family Devotions and Family Prayer
Family Projects to Help Others

"Parents play a vital role in the faith development of their children and teenagers. In fact, what happens in the home is probably more powerful than anything that happens in a Sunday school class, confirmation program, or youth group."

"Congregations at Crossroads: A National Study of Adults and Youth in the Lutheran Church—Missouri Synod." The study was done by Search Institute, Minneapolis, MN, 1996, 21.

Joshua's generation was faithful to God. Moses' generation had passed on that faith to Joshua's generation. How successful was Joshua's generation at leaving a legacy of faith?

> *After a while the people of Joshua's generation died, and the next generation did not know the LORD or any of the things he had done for Israel.*

> *The LORD had brought their ancestors out of Egypt, and they had worshiped him. But now the Israelites stopped worshiping the LORD and worshiped the idols of Baal and Astarte, as well as the idols of other gods from nearby nations. The LORD was so angry.... (Ju 2:10-11).*

Something went wrong! Was there a consequence? Yes, without a legacy of faith the children of Joshua's generation, the grandchildren of Moses' generation, inherited moral relativism. *And everyone did what they thought was right (Ju 21:25b).*

The King James Version of the Bible puts it this way: *Every man did that which was right in his own eyes.* In other words, if it feels good, it is the right thing to do. If it is right for you, then it is moral. It does not matter what you believe as long as you are sincere. Does that sound like life in the United States today? Like Moses' and Joshua's generations, we are one generation away from losing our children to the Christian faith. Homegrown faith coupled with a strong participation in a local congregation is the remedy.

Parental Love Wipes Out a Multitude of Sins

Every parent makes mistakes now and again. Please do not turn away from nurturing Christian faith in your children, including your teenage children, because you might make mistakes. You will make mistakes! You will feel inadequate. You will get questions that you can't answer. You will sense your lack of spiritual maturity.

The Apostle Peter tells us that *love wipes away many sins (1 Pe 4:8).* We have watched how our two children have responded to our mistakes, our failures, and our imperfections as we have parented them in love. They overlook them. Our children love us because we first loved them just as we love God because He first loved us (see 1 Jo 4:19). It is the love you have and express toward your children that saves the day. Solomon expressed it this way: *Hatred stirs up trouble; love overlooks the wrongs that others do (Pr 10:12).* Assuming you grew up in a home where love was expressed deeply and genuinely, you can think of examples where you overlooked your parents' mistakes. Why? Because love really does wipe away wrongs.

Love your kids. Experiment with the ideas and strategies found in this book. God will honor whatever efforts you make, in spite of your failures. God calls each of us as parents to be faithful to the "Deuteronomy Promise," leaving the results up to God.

A Bible Passage to Remember

> *Moses said to the people: Attention, Israel! GOD, our God! GOD the one and only!*
>
> *Love GOD, your God, with your whole heart: love him with all that's in you, love him with all you've got!*
>
> *Write these commandments that I've given you today on your hearts. Get them inside of you and then get them inside your children. Talk about them wherever you are, sitting at home or walking in the street; talk about them from the time you get up in the morning to when you fall into bed at night.*
>
> *That's why GOD commanded us to follow all these rules, so that we would live reverently before GOD, our God, as he gives us this good life, keeping us alive for a long time to come.*
>
> *It will be a set-right and put-together life for us if we make sure that we do this entire commandment in the Presence of GOD, our God, just as he commanded us to do (De 6:4-7, 24-25 THE MESSAGE).*

A Thought to Consider

No matter where you are in your spiritual journey, no matter how little or how much you know about the Bible, no matter how busy your schedule, you *can* nurture your kids in the Christian faith. Faith is caught within the normal routines of family life.

A Question to Ask Yourself

What do your children catch from you? Faith? Materialism? Indulgence?

Dialogue Questions for Group Study

Jumpstart a healthy homegrown faith dialogue in your Sunday school class or small group with the following questions. You also can use the "A Bible Passage to Remember," "A Thought to Consider," and "A Question to Ask Yourself" at the end of each chapter to spark a lively discussion.

1. How does the "Deuteronomy Promise" give you hope as a parent?
2. How does the reality of research on faith and values formation dispel the myth that parents have little influence on their kids' faith and values? Have you been misled as a parent by pop psychology and conventional wisdom?
3. How are we one generation away from losing our children to Christianity? What will you do about it?
4. How are you qualified to pass on the faith to your children and grandchildren?
5. How are your congregation's ministries supplementing your homegrown faith?

Chapter Two

The Top Ten HomeGrown Faith Practices for Parents

Parents, don't be hard on your children. Raise them properly.

Teach them and instruct them about the Lord (Ep 6:4).

The Goodman Family

Joey carefully lifted the picture frame, dusted under it, then set it back down again on the coffee table. Dusting was one of his jobs when he stayed with Grandma Anna. She thought that boys, not just girls, should know how to clean. Joey's brother Matt had learned how to dust and now it was his turn. Matt had finished his chores and watched as Joey dusted.

Joey didn't particularly like doing chores, but he did like being with Grandma Anna. Stuff like dusting wasn't hard to do, but he had to be very careful because Grandma had lots of "pretties." These were fragile things that needed to be dusted. He also had to dust under them, a concept that Joey never understood. He thought, *If they were never picked up, how could anyone tell if there was dust under them?* Some were really old pictures of her parents and grandparents and of her and grandpa together before he died. She also had newer pictures of Joey and Matt and their parents.

Joey carefully picked up his grandma and grandpa's wedding picture. "I like this picture, Grandma." He held it carefully. "You look really pretty, but you sure did dress funny back then."

"We thought we were pretty hot stuff," Grandma Anna said.

Joey laughed at his grandmother's description. "It's hard to think of you as young. How old were you when this was taken?"

"I was 20 and your grandpa was 21 years old," she replied.

"You were married forever! I bet you miss him a lot," Matt said as he did the mental math. They had been married for 40 years before his grandpa died two years ago. Sometimes his grandma talked like he was still around.

"Yes, I do miss him." She smiled. "I'm glad I will see him again when I get to heaven."

"Is Grandpa in heaven?" Joey asked.

"Oh, yes. He's there."

Studying the picture, Matt asked, "Daddy said Grandpa was really close to God. What does that mean?"

"It means that he talked to God a lot and read his Bible," she answered. "He loved to listen to worship music, too. He would always hum songs."

"Did he teach Daddy to pray?" asked Joey.

"Yes. We prayed together every day and read the Bible, too," she said.

"Is that why you do it with us?" Matt asked.

"Of course," Anna said. "I want you and Joey to learn how to get closer to God."

Joey climbed into her lap. "Just like Grandpa."

"Yes." Anna gave him a tight hug. "Just like Grandpa."

The Davis Family

"Hi, Mom," Chris said as he answered the phone. He knew the call would be from his mom because it was 3:30 p.m., and she always called then to make sure they were home from school.

Bonnie laughed. "Hey, smarty. You think you know me so well. It would have been pretty funny if you would have said 'Hello, Mom' to your coach."

"Yeah, he would get a laugh out of that, but I can usually count on it being you checking in on us."

"You know I always like to see if you have gotten home safely. I worry," his mom said.

"Don't worry. We all got home OK. I did talk to someone on the way from the bus stop though."

"Oh?" Bonnie's 'Mom radar' went on full alert.

"Yeah. You know the little old lady who lives on the corner. We sometimes see her working in her yard."

"I think her name is Mrs. Jenkins," Bonnie said.

"That's it," said Chris. "Anyway, she wanted to know if I could help her with her yard work some time. She said she would pay me."

"That sounds like a great idea. Let's talk about it more when I get home."

"OK, Mom," said Chris. "Talk to you later."

Later that evening, Chris asked his mom, "Mom, can we talk about the job with Mrs. Jenkins now?"

"What job?" his father asked.

"Mrs. Jenkins, the lady who lives down the street, asked Chris if he could help her with her yard work," Bonnie explained.

"That's great, Chris," his dad said. "I had a job when I was your age. You can start saving some money."

"She's really nice, Mom," said Chris.

Bonnie asked, "What about your homework?"

"Mrs. Jenkins was a teacher, so she knows school is important. She said that if working affected my grades, I would have to stop until I get caught up," Chris said.

"Then I think it sounds like a good thing for both of you."

"Yes!" Chris jumped up to hug his parents. "Can I go call Mrs. Jenkins? She gave me her phone number."

"Go ahead," his dad said. "She probably needs you to work as soon as possible."

Chris called Mrs. Jenkins, and they decided that Thursdays after school would be the best time for both of them. Chris didn't usually have homework on Thursday nights, and Mrs. Jenkins could be home that day to tell him the things she needed done.

The following Thursday, Chris rode his bike to Mrs. Jenkins' house. He really didn't need to ride his bike, but somehow it made him feel more like he was going to work than if he just walked. Chris rang the doorbell, but there was no answer. His heart sank. *Had she forgotten?* Chris decided to walk to the side of the house in case he could see her in the back yard.

"There you are, Chris," Mrs. Jenkins said. "Right on time. I thought I would get us a little head start."

Chris thought he would hate to see what Mrs. Jenkins called a big start. All around her were branches she had clipped off her large bougainvillea plants.

He grinned. "It doesn't look like you need my help."

"Sure I do," she said as she climbed down from the stepladder. "Your job is to cut those branches into smaller pieces and stuff them into the bags over there." She gestured to a box of heavy-duty trash bags. "Then you can haul them to the trash cans out back."

"OK." Chris headed toward the pile of branches.

"Here are your clippers, and I got you some new gloves. The stickers on the bougainvilleas are really sharp."

"Thanks." Chris pulled on his new gloves, grabbed a trash bag, and began to cut pieces of the branches into it.

After several minutes, Mrs. Jenkins looked over at him. "You're a quiet one. I've had some kids work with me who have talked my ear off."

"There are other kids?" Chris looked around her yard. There didn't seem to be that much work to have other kids helping, too.

"Not now. Now it's just you. But three others worked for me in the past. The last one just turned 16, and he needed to get a job that had more hours so that he could pay for his gas and car insurance. He just started driving, and I think it cost him a little more than he expected."

"Oh." Chris didn't really know how to answer. He thought he would be working *for* Mrs. Jenkins not *with* her. Being a shy person, it was sometimes hard for Chris to come up with the right words in a conversation.

Sensing his discomfort, Mrs. Jenkins moved right along with the conversation. "So, Chris, where do you go to church?"

Chris tied the first bag. "I go with my mom to Grace Church."

"Just you and your mom?" She moved to the next bush.

"No. My brother and sister come, too. And my Dad goes sometimes."

Mrs. Jenkins could tell that Chris was uncomfortable talking about his Dad not going to church. "What's your favorite part about going to church?"

"I dunno," he mumbled. "I guess it would be the stories and the music."

"Mine, too," said Mrs. Jenkins.

"What kind of teacher were you?"

"I've taught a few different things." Mrs. Jenkins finished another bush. "I was a middle-school English teacher." She smiled when Chris made a face. "I also taught history for a while."

"I like history. What else?" He closed another bag.

"I've been a Sunday school teacher for almost forty years. I think I enjoy that the most."

"How come?" Chris wondered why someone would enjoy Sunday school so much.

"Because I like telling people about Jesus," Mrs. Jenkins said. "But we don't have to be in Sunday school to talk about Him. I like talking about Him all the time. In fact, you can ask me any question you want about the Bible. If I can't answer it, I'll try to find the answer for you."

"Cool." Chris really did have a few questions that he had been too shy to ask his Sunday school teachers.

Mrs. Jenkins straightened up and rubbed the small of her back. "That's enough for today. You did a great job. When you come next week, I'll make us a snack." She reached into her pocket. "Here's your money."

"Gee, thanks!" Chris took the ten-dollar bill. "See you next week!"

Could You Do This?

"That concert was amazing," Dan said to his mom. "Thanks for taking me."

Liz hadn't planned to spend her evening near huge speakers, but she had to admit that she enjoyed the music. Who knew a Christian band could be so good? "What? I can't hear you," she called out, teasing her son.

"Mom." Dan drawled the word in his soon-to-be teenager tone of voice.

"Okay, okay," she said. "I liked it. The bands seemed really sincere about what they were singing about."

"Yeah," said Dan. "The words were cool."

"Haven't I heard the choir sing some of those songs at church?" Liz asked. "They seemed pretty familiar."

"Yeah," said Dan, nodding, "some churches are using a lot of their songs. Can I put the CD on while we drive home?"

To her son, she said, "Sure," but to the Lord, she said, "Thank you."

The Collins Family

"Wait!" Liz called to the backs of the men in her family as they walked toward the door. "What about dinner?"

"No time, honey," said Sam. "I have to get the boys to the soccer field. Warm-ups start at six." Both boys were on soccer teams, and they spent most of their evenings at practice. Now that Sam was helping coach Louie's team, he was almost never around either.

"But, Sam, we haven't had dinner together in over a week. Carla is actually going to be home tonight, and I hoped that we could sit down at the table together."

"Come on, Liz," said Sam. "It's not like I want to be away from home at dinner time, but we have made commitments to the team. We both decided that soccer would be good for the boys."

"Don't worry, Mom," Louie said. "We'll grab a burger on the way to practice."

"See?" Sam gave his wife a quick hug. "I'm going to feed them, and you and Carla can have a nice meal together."

"It's not about the food," said Liz.

Sam paused. "I know. We'll work on it, OK? Maybe next week we can eat together."

Carla heard this as she entered the kitchen. "Nope. I have try-outs for the school play next week. They start at five."

"We gotta go, Dad!" Dan opened the door. "Bye, Mom, Carla."

Liz sighed. "How do families who eat together find the time to do it? There are just too many things going on."

"Beats me." Carla opened a cabinet and reached for a glass. "What's for dinner?"

Making the Time

Grandma Anna is practicing the ways of faith at home with her grandkids just as she did with her son while he was growing up. Homegrown faith is a normal part of her routine. Mrs. Jenkins is practicing the ways of faith at home to neighborhood kids she hires. She has been part of a congregation long enough to know that kids need Christian mentors. The Collins family is trying to share meals together. All three families are illustrating practices from the "Top Ten Faith Practices for Parents," which are biblically grounded, research-based faith practices critical for parents and grandparents as they pass on the faith to the next generation.

Think about it. We work with our kids as they practice piano. We haul our kids to soccer practice. We struggle with them as they practice their multiplication exercises. Why not practice our faith at home? If we want our children to be people of faith as adults, then we must practice the ways of faith at home now.

Martin Luther wrote his *Small Catechism* as a tool for parents to practice the ways of faith with their children at home. His work included explanations of the Ten Commandments, the Apostles' Creed, the Lord's Prayer, baptism, confession, morning and evening prayers, and mealtime prayers. Read what he writes about moms and dads:

> Most certainly father and mother are apostles, bishops, and priests to their children, for it is they who make them acquainted with the Gospel. In short, there is no greater or noble authority on earth than that of parents over their children, for this authority is both spiritual and temporal. Whoever teaches the gospel to another is truly his apostle and bishop.[3]

Parents, your ministry with your children and teenagers is a calling that only you can fully accomplish. Your practice of the ways of faith at home with your children sets the stage for their relationship with Jesus Christ as adults. We have created a simple inventory of faith practices you can observe with your children and teenagers. We hope these practices will be as helpful to you as they have been with our family.

Top Ten HomeGrown Faith Practices for Parents*

Let's start with an inventory of the faith practices in your home. Place a number from the Opinion Scale on the line before each statement that best describes what you sense is

[3] Martin Luther, *The Estate of Marriage*, http://www.warwick.ac.uk/fac/arts/History/teaching/protref/women/WR0913.htm

happening in your family. This inventory is not a test; rather, it gives you a big picture of the strength and growth areas in your family.

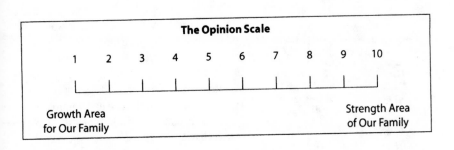

____ 1. **Personal Devotions.** My child** sees me praying and reading the Bible on a regular basis.

____ 2. **Family Devotions.** I read the Bible or have devotions with my child** at least once a week.

____ 3. **Caring Conversations.** My child** and I talk together often about how our Christian faith relates to everyday life.

____ 4. **Family Rituals and Traditions.** I create rituals and traditions that identify my family to be like Jesus.

____ 5. **Family Worship.** My child** and I regularly participate in meaningful worship with our congregation.

____ 6. **Family Prayer.** My child** and I pray together daily.

____ 7. **Family Acts of Service.** My child** and I engage often in acts of service within our home and join together in community service at least once every four months.

____ 8. **Blessings.** I communicate often to my child** that God and I love and appreciate him/her.

____ 9. **Relationships with Caring Adults.** I create opportunities for my child** to form healthy, personal trusted relationships with people of faith of all ages.

____ 10. **Shared Mealtimes***.** Our family eats a meal together without interruptions (no TV, video games, phone) at least five times each week.

____ **TOTAL SCORE OUT OF POSSIBLE 100**

*"Parents" includes parents, grandparents, and other primary caregivers in the household.

**"Child" includes teenagers.

***Practices 2, 3, 4, 6, 7, and 8 can be done easily during family mealtimes.

Parents Matter: Television

A look at the research

A survey of 394 parents and their second- through sixth-grade children studied three strategies parents used to manage their children's television viewing of violent programming. The three strategies—talking with children about violent television programs, restricting or limiting television viewing, and watching television with children—had different effects upon the children.

Popular parenting advice today often encourages parents to watch violent programs with their children. This survey suggested that children who view violent programs with their parents picked up the message that their parents approved of this programming. Parents who disapprove may want to avoid viewing violent programs with their kids. Instead, they ought to consider restricting the viewing of violent programming. If a parent chooses to view violent programs with their children, we recommend they talk about the violence with their children and their disapproval of it.

Talking with children about violent programming was found to have mixed results. Simply talking about the content of violent television programming did not necessarily restrict their access to such programming; sometimes the children perceived parental approval.

Parents need to understand their reactions toward television have a dramatic effect on their children's attitude.

A. I. Nathanson, "Parent and child perspectives on the presence and meaning of parental television mediation," *Journal of Broadcasting & Electronic Media*, 45, 2001, 210-220.

Personal Devotions

My child sees me praying and reading the Bible on a regular basis.

Imagine if people could learn only from the consequences of their own actions. It would take children hours to learn anything, and they would most likely not survive their adolescence! Fortunately, much of human learning is a result of observation. We watch the actions of others—especially people we love, trust, admire, or respect—and incorporate what they do into our own behaviors. We observe this personally or through the media (television, video, books, magazines, etc.). Research into how people learn has demonstrated the power and effectiveness of role modeling.[4]

How does this translate into a faith practice for parents and grandparents? Let your kids and grandkids "catch" you praying and reading the Bible. Years ago Kathy and I would read a short passage of Scripture, talk about it, and then pray. This morning routine, behind a closed door in our bedroom, had always been a practice that strengthened our faith and our marriage. One day, we realized that this faith practice needed to be done openly so our children could see the importance we placed on reading the Bible and praying together. We moved our devotional time to our kitchen table. We said nothing to our kids, who were young at the time, about what we were doing. We continue the practice to this day. Our kids have never asked why we do this, though they see the routine five times a week. We do not need to whisper a word about our actions. Our modeling of Bible reading and prayer speaks louder than any words we could say.

Family Devotions

I read the Bible or have devotions with my child at least once a week.

[4] This research was popularized by Albert Bandura, beginning with his work on children imitating aggressive, violent behavior.

"Aaaw, do we have to do devotions right now? I was just starting to have fun." Is this what you hear after calling your children for family devotions? Your family will never beg you to do devotions. You cannot wait for a ground swell of enthusiasm to come from your kids before you begin. You can make family devotions a normal part of your family's routine, making them easier and fun to do. Here's how to get and keep devotions going and growing in your family.

Keep it within the normal routines of family life. Family devotions only need to take a few minutes a day. An entire evening with the family is rare today, and we need to find a way to work family devotions into an already existing family routine like bedtime or mealtime. A few minutes each day is worth the effort.

Keep it simple. Family devotions can involve reading a passage of Scripture and commenting on its meaning. Family devotions can be reading a story and Bible verse from a devotional book, or an age-appropriate Bible at bedtime. Talk about your favorite Bible verses or read a Christian book together (C. S. Lewis' *The Chronicles of Narnia* were a big hit with our kids, for instance).

Keep it kid-friendly. Ask your kids to choose what they would like to do for family devotions. Your children and teenagers will be more engaged in family devotions if they have a say in the activity.

Keep it real. Your devotional activity needs to relate to the real world of your kids. Do not try a presentation on the hypostatic union of Christ. Ask your children what they would like to discuss.

Keep it mixed up. There is no perfect way to do family devotions. This gives you permission to change what you do and where you do it. We have done devotions on our back porch, in the car, and in a swimming pool.

Keep it working. If what you're doing does not work, try something else.

Keep it moving. That means no lectures. Give everyone a chance to talk, and ask them open-ended questions rather than yes/no questions.

Keep it fun. Laughter is good for the soul.

Keep it going when you are out. Take devotions to restaurants or other places when you go out.

Caring Conversations

My child and I talk often about how our Christian faith relates to everyday life.

"Could you pick up the towels off the bathroom floor? And remember to take out the trash." This is maintenance talk. Every family needs this kind of talk to keep the family going. Families also need caring conversations: positive, meaningful communication about the real issues of life—concerns, fears, joys, frustrations, beliefs. Positive family communication is a characteristic of strong families.[5] Faith talk needs to be part of that positive communication. Discussions about Jesus, prayer, forgiveness, grace, and other faith topics help connect God to everyday life. If the followers of the faith in the Old Testament and New Testament never talked with their families about the faith, where would we be today?

Children are often the ones to initiate faith conversations. One study found that chil-

---

5 Nick Stinnett and John DeFrain, *Secrets of Strong Families* (Boston: Little, Brown, 1985).

dren, rather than their parents, triggered 65 to 78 percent of faith conversations.[6] These conversations usually began with a question, and they occurred in the evening at mealtime and bedtime. Interestingly, these faith conversations were not prompted by Sunday school or worship service experiences. Unfortunately, most parents in the study did not strongly sense that they had communicated their beliefs to their children.

What can we learn from this study? As parents, we need to be unmistakably intentional about caring conversations in general. In particular, caring faith conversations with our children can clearly communicate our faith and values. These conversations need to occur daily and cover a wide variety of meaningful and important topics.

Family Rituals and Traditions

I create rituals and traditions that identify my family as one wanting to be like Jesus.

Thanksgiving, Advent, Christmas, Lent, Easter, New Year's, the Fourth of July, birthdays, anniversaries, baptisms, weddings, funerals, mealtimes, bedtimes, vacations—all of these are opportunities to build closeness with your family. Rituals and traditions communicate family values, bind generations together, encourage mutual support, and provide continuity and stability to life. They help families identify themselves as Christian, afford them the opportunity to enjoy time together, and offer a valuable way to pass on the faith to the next generation.

What rituals and traditions do you already practice that identify your family as one wanting to be like Jesus? How can you change other rituals and traditions you already have to identify your family as one wanting to be like Jesus? What new rituals and traditions do you need to create?

Family Worship

My child and I regularly participate together in meaningful worship with our congregation.

Children can worship with other children. And children's church programs can be a positive spiritual experience for your kids unless they take the place of corporate worship. Youth worship services are healthy and great opportunities for teenagers to worship together, unless these experiences take the place of corporate worship. Families need to worship together regularly with a congregation, though not necessarily sit together.

"But," you say, "my kids don't get anything out of my congregation's worship service." You do not take your kids into congregational worship just for them to get something out of it. You also take them to watch adults get something out of it. Worship as a family.

Family Prayer

My child and I pray together daily.

We have noticed that many people view prayer as a chore—something they are obligated to do. Others view prayer as a classroom course—all they have to do is get the

[6] Christ Boyatzis and Denise Janicki, "Parent-Child Communication About Religion: Survey and Diary Data on Unilateral Transmission and Bi-directional Reciprocity Styles," *Review of Religious Research* 44.3 (2003): 252-279.

right technique, the correct heart attitude, the appropriate words, and then God might give them an "A" (give them what they asked for). Still others see prayer as spiritual exercise—four more, three more, two more, one more, "Wow, aren't I spiritual?" Finally, we know some people who see prayer as an S.O.S.—something you do when you are in a crisis or emergency.

What might happen instead if we viewed prayer from the point of view of God's character—a loving, caring God ready, with open arms, to listen to our every need? Even more, what might happen if we prayed with our children every day?

> *Jesus understands every weakness of ours, because he was tempted in every way that we are. But he did not sin! So whenever we are in need, we should come bravely before the throne of our merciful God. There we will be treated with undeserved kindness, and we will find help (He 4:15-16).*

The following question was posed to 3,290 teenagers, ages 13-17, as part of a larger study[7] on the religious lives of American teenagers: "In the last year, have you prayed out loud or silently together with one or both of your parents, other than at mealtimes or at religious services?"

Just over 40 percent of the teens answered "yes." When only Protestant families were examined, the percentage answering yes jumped to nearly half the teens.

Have you prayed with your kids in the last year outside of mealtimes or congregational functions? When compared across Protestant denominations, distinct differences emerged. Look at the percentage of teens who reported praying with a parent within the last year. Where does your family stand?

Denomination	Percent of Teens Who Pray with Parents
Assemblies of God	63
Disciples of Christ	33
Episcopal Church USA	35
Evangelical Lutheran Church USA	32
Lutheran Church Missouri Synod	46
Presbyterian Church USA	33
Southern Baptist Convention	56
United Methodist Church	34
National Baptist	62
Church of God in Christ	70
Conservative Protestant	51
Mainline Protestant	32
Black Protestant	53

[7] Phil Schwadel and Christian Smith, "Portraits of Protestant Teens: A Report on Teenagers in Major U.S. Denominations," *National Study of Youth and Religion*. (Chapel Hill: University of North Carolina Press, 2005).

Acts of Service

My child and I engage often in acts of service within our home and join in community service at least once every four months.

Serving others as a family was found to be a significant faith practice of parents who were serious about passing on the faith to their children.[8] Why is this an important faith practice? In Jesus' time, there was a sect of Judaism that focused on a strict interpretation of the Hebrew laws. One such Pharisee, perhaps wanting to debate Jesus, asked Him to name God's most important commandment. Jesus answered, *Love the Lord your God with all your heart, soul, and mind (Ma 22:37)*. Before the Pharisee could counter, Jesus continued, *The second most important commandment is like this one. And it is, 'Love others as much as you love yourself.' All the Law of Moses and the Books of the Prophets are based on these two commandments (Ma 22:39-40)*.

Family acts of service fulfill Jesus' second commandment. They put legs on our homegrown faith. James, the half-brother of Jesus, said, *Faith that doesn't lead us to do good deeds is all alone and dead (Jam 2:17)!*

Blessings

I communicate often to my children that they are loved and appreciated by me and by God.

Creation began with God's blessing. He wanted nothing but good to come from the cosmos.

Then he gave the living creatures his blessing—he told the ocean creatures to live everywhere in the ocean and the birds to live everywhere on earth (Ge 1:22).

God continued with blessings after creating people. He intended for people to prosper in relationship with Him. Would it not have been silly for God to create the world then pronounce a curse upon it? A curse would have been contrary to God's nature.

So God created humans to be like himself; he made men and women. God gave them his blessing and said: Have a lot of children! Fill the earth with people and bring it under your control. Rule over the fish in the ocean, the birds in the sky, and every animal on the earth (Ge 1:27-28).

The Old Testament is full of examples of blessings as well as curses. Parents have the power to bless or curse their children. Parents can desire and express approval and good fortune upon their children or they can belittle and put them down.

	Blessings			Curses	
Accepting	Encouraging	Recognizing	Invective	Sarcastic	Disparaging
Loving	Freeing	Forgiving	Insolent	Castigating	Critical
Reassuring	Building up	Inviting	Belittling	Condemning	Judgmental

What memories do you have of growing up? Were you blessed or cursed by your parents? Did you have a mom or dad who built you up or tore you down?

---

[8] "Congregations at Crossroads: A National Study of Adults and Youth in the Lutheran Church—Missouri Synod." (Minneapolis: Search Institute, 1996).

- "He was always pointing out what I did wrong."
- "Why did she constantly put me down?"
- "He never could tell me he loved me."
- "I sat at my father's grave trying to forgive him. Today I still feel his thumb on my back!"

The above statements are those of adult children describing the curses they received from their parents. What about blessings?

- "My dad would say things like, 'We are so fortunate to have you in our family!'"
- "I knew my mom was proud of me no matter what."
- "'Hey, sweetie, I love you!' That's how Dad still greets me on the phone."

Are you raising your kids through blessings? The Bible directs us, as we are raising our children, to watch for insulting, invective language and treatment of our kids.

Parents, don't be hard on your children. Raise them properly. Teach them and instruct them about the Lord (Ep 6:4).

Research also supports blessing our children. One of the characteristics of strong families is the expression of appreciation and affection for each other.[9] Bless your kids every day—before they leave home with notes in their lunch sacks, by phone calls in the afternoon, when you pick them up in the evening, at mealtime as you engage in caring conversation, and at bedtime before they fall asleep.

Relationships with Caring Adults

I create opportunities for my child to form healthy, personal, trusted relationships with people of faith of all ages.

Kids need more than their parents passing on the faith. The *National Study of Youth and Religion*, mentioned in Chapter One, found that the most religiously devoted teenagers had the largest number of non-parent adults in their lives

[9] Stinnett and DeFrain, *Secrets of Strong Families.*

Could You Do This?

"It's time," thought Anna as she looked at the clothes in the closet. Many of them had belonged to her late husband, and until now she just hadn't had the heart to get rid of them. She sighed as she touched the sleeve of one of the soft shirts.

"What's the matter, Grandma," Matt asked. "Why are you so sad?"

"I was just missing your Grandpa." She sighed. "But I was also thinking that there are a lot of clothes in this closet that someone could be using."

"Who?"

"Do you remember when I told you that I was going to start working at the homeless shelter that our church helps?" Matt nodded and she continued. "Well, I found out yesterday that they really are in need of men's clothes. I had a little talk with God on the way home ..."

Matt smiled, knowing that Grandma's little talks with God meant that she was praying.

"...and I think that the Lord was telling me that helping others by giving them Grandpa's clothes was a better way to remember him than just letting them hang in the closet."

"Won't you miss them?" Matt knew that having Grandpa's clothes around helped her remember him.

"Oh, I'll keep a few of my favorites."

"Like his old red shirt that you always wanted him to throw away?"

"That ...and maybe this old jacket." Anna reached out and stroked the well-worn leather. "But I think it's time that we put his other things and clothes that I'm not wearing to good use."

"I bet we have stuff at home that we could give," said Matt.

"Probably." His grandmother smiled. "Just make sure that it's okay with your mom first."

who encouraged them and offered advice or help.[10] The parents of these devoted teenagers were also more likely than the parents of less religiously devoted teenagers to know about and talk with these supportive adults.

Kids need at least three Christian adults in their lives who practice a vibrant, vital faith to help them grow in their relationship with God.[11] Parents and grandparents can be decidedly instrumental in creating such opportunities for relationships with older Christians. In the stories of our three families, Mrs. Jenkins was one such mentor. The research speaks to the need for these intergenerational relationships that nurture faith. Within your congregation are many opportunities to connect your children and teenagers with adults who will talk with them, encourage them, and teach them the ways of faith.

Shared Mealtimes

Our family eats a meal together without interruptions (no television, video games, phone, etc.) at least five times each week.

Our grandparents would laugh if they knew how much money researchers spend to discover that the most effective strategies parents, grandparents, and other primary caregivers have for raising healthy, well-adjusted kids is to eat meals together frequently. The family mealtime is making a comeback! It is the most important meal you will eat because you are sharing it with those closest to you.

One nationally recognized study found that teenagers from families who ate meals together five or more times a week were less likely to smoke, drink, or use marijuana than young people who shared meals less frequently.[12] However, eating meals with your kids five times a week presents some genuinely difficult obstacles. We understand. We have two teenagers who are competitive athletes, work part-time, participate in the youth ministry, study hard, and the list goes on. Sometimes we have to eat at 10:00 p.m.—it's that important! Researchers continue to gather the benefits of shared mealtimes, from building stronger family relationships to higher academic achievement.

[10] Smith and Denton, *Soul Searching*, 226.

[11] Roland Martinson, preliminary research for "The Study of Exemplary Congregations in Youth Ministry," *www.faithfactors.com*.

[12] "The Importance of Family Dinners," The National Center on Addiction and Substance Abuse at Columbia University, 2003.

If you are not currently sharing meals together, start with one meal each week and work your way up to five. Your hard work will pay off.

If you review the "Top Ten Faith Practices," you will see that "Family Devotions," "Caring Conversations," "Family Rituals and Traditions," and "Family Acts of Service" all can be practiced during your shared mealtimes.

Finding the Time

You do not need to add "doing God" to your "To Do" list. You can nurture Christian faith in your family through normal routines of family life. If Moses could re-write Deuteronomy 6:5, he might say,

> . . . and make talking with your kids, including your teenagers, an everyday occurrence. When you are driving them to soccer practice, pray for the people involved in that car accident along the road. While you're eating out, ask a question that gets a faith conversation going. In the morning, before everyone leaves for the day, circle up the family and say a fifteen-second prayer. In the evening, while loading the dishwasher, ask a family member to read a Bible verse.

It really is about making your Christian faith a normal part of your everyday life. You do not have to find the time to nurture your family's faith; you weave it into the 168 hours each week that you and everyone else have been given.

Holiday Time

Any holiday can be an excellent time to reinforce your family's values and commitment to the Lord. Because this is a time when extended families often come together, your children can have the opportunity to view the bigger picture, that they come from a larger group of people who want to be more like Jesus.

One-on-One Time

One-on-one time is just you and your child. Perhaps you take a walk or sit on a bench enjoying an ice cream cone. What a great time to read a short passage from the Bible and pray together, or talk about what Jesus is doing in your lives.

Bedtime

"Now I lay me down to sleep . . ." Sound familiar? For many of us, this was the way we said our prayers at bedtime. You can make bedtime prayers a ritual in your home in the same way. Start from the day you bring your child home from the hospital. As you hold your baby close, thank God for him and ask for His protection before putting him in his crib. Toddlers can learn to say the simple "Now I lay me down to sleep . . ." type of prayer. As you listen to his prayers each night, you will be teaching him that this is a special time for him to spend with God. As your child gets older, move from these simple prayers to one where your child mentions specific needs or reasons for giving thanks. Allow an older child to pray on his own so that it becomes part of his nightly routine, not just one you encourage. Turn the tables on a teenage child. Ask him to tuck you into bed and say a prayer for you.

Family Time

"Let's do something together as a family. What do you want to do tonight?" You could see a movie, play miniature golf, or go on a picnic together. No matter what you decide to do as a family, include nurturing faith into the activity. Discuss the movie on the way home. Ask if family values were depicted in positive or negative ways. If your child gets a hole-in-one during your game of miniature golf, it becomes a perfect time for a hug and to say, "I love you." On a picnic, it only takes a second to ask your family to stop and look around at the scenery and thank God for the beautiful world He made.

Drive Time

Do you spend a lot of time in the car with your kids? Start a faith tradition by praying any time you get in the car with your family. Take turns praying that God will give you a safe journey. It will soon become as routine as putting on your seatbelt; a habit that will continue when your children are driving.

Getting a driver's license is a glorious right of passage for a young person and a mixed blessing for her parents. You want her to drive and be independent, but you are anxious every time she pulls out of the driveway. Celebrate this milestone with a prayer of thanksgiving. You can also ask for God's protection as she takes on this new responsibility. Whenever she uses the car, take a moment to pray together that God will bring her home safely.

Mealtime

"Dear God, thanks for the food. Amen. Let's eat." Sometimes, prayer is seen as something that stands in the way of us and the food. The quicker the prayer, the quicker we can eat. Do not panic! We are not encouraging you to pray for all of your congregation's missionaries by name before you can eat. However, you can incorporate faith into mealtimes in many ways. Involve your family in meal preparation. Not only is it good for other family members to know how to put a meal together, but it also gives you time to share your day. This can also be time to focus on the food you will be eating. You can say simple things like, "How amazing that God made so many varieties of food for us," or "I appreciate the microwave; I don't know how I'd cook without it." Use this as a problem-solving time or encouragement time, a time to bring your family closer together and closer to God. And before you eat, thank God again for the food He has provided.

Vacation Time

"Where should we go on vacation this year?" This probably doesn't sound like a time to talk about faith issues, but it can be a great opportunity for you to nurture your family's faith. It could be a simple prayer thanking God for the resources to take a vacation. Or it could be a time to work together as you choose where you want to go. On a recent trip to the Grand Canyon, our family stood and marveled at God's creation. This could happen for your family too, at the beach or the mountains. Watching a beautiful sunset together and saying, "Thank you, Lord" can show your family's gratitude for God's creation and bring a beautiful end to the day.

Illness

"Mommy, I feel sick." Being sick is no fun, but you can turn it into a special time with your child. After tending to the physical needs of your child, it is time to address the spiritual ones. A kiss on the forehead and the words "I love you" sometimes feel better than comfy pajamas and a glass of cool water. Take the time to pray over your child. Give him the opportunity to pray if he feels up to it. Let him tell God how crummy he feels and ask God to help him feel better. Read him a Bible story or sing a favorite song. Tell him stories from your childhood when you got sick and what made you feel better. His body may still feel crummy, but he will know you and God love him very much.

Teaching Time

What are teaching times? They are moments you can use to share a family value with your child. They happen all the time; we just have to train ourselves to look for them. Here are a few examples. A cashier gives you too much change back; you hear someone using inappropriate language; you see something on television that goes against your values. Your child learns from what you do and how you respond. A few words such as, "I think we better tell the cashier she made a mistake," "I'm glad we don't use those words," or "I don't think I want to watch a program that shows people hurting each other" teach your child in ways that a sermon or lecture never could.

After-school Time

If you are not home, do you call your child to check in when school is out? This can be a stressful time for children and parents. Set up a time when you call your child (or have her call you) and ask about her day. Help her solve any situations she is concerned about, and tell her how much you and God love her.

Activity Time

You can do chores together, play games, hike, or bicycle. Whatever you do together can be a time to nurture your family's faith. While you are doing the chores around the house, play worship music to make the tasks more enjoyable. When playing games, you can encourage each other and be good sports. When you are outside together, even an occasional comment about the beauty of God's creation will remind family members of God's love.

Errands/Shopping Time

"I have errands to run today, does anyone want to go with me?" Running errands or going shopping can be the perfect time to talk to your children. The time you spend in the car is a great opportunity to learn about each other or just be together. Don't feel that you have to fill every moment with conversation. Before you start your journey, pray with your child that you will have a safe trip. Be sure to thank God for the good company.

Television Time

"Turn off that junk" is what many of us probably want to say when we watch television. But TV watching can be entertaining and educational if you plan what you watch beforehand. At the beginning of the week, decide how much time you want to spend watching television. Then sit down with your family and look through your local listings. Check out movies, sports, and entertainment programs your family would like to watch. If you choose to watch a movie or show with which you are unfamiliar, commit to turning it off if it becomes inappropriate. Talk with your family about taking control of the television and not letting the television control your family. When you are finished, take a moment to pray with your family. Thank God that you have the opportunity to have this kind of entertainment, and ask for His wisdom in choosing appropriate programs to watch.

Ministry Time

Is there an opportunity for you to minister in your child's youth group or Sunday school class? Congregations are always looking for good people to volunteer their time and talents. But often parents are reluctant to minister in a group where their child is involved. "It would make me (or him or her) uncomfortable if I had to do any disciplining." The answer to that is to speak with the other adults in the class about your concerns, and ask them to take charge of disciplining your child, should the need arise.

Celebration Time

It's time to party! Whether it's a birthday or anniversary, your family enjoys a good celebration. You can use this time to nurture your family's faith. Ask God's blessing on the celebration and on the people involved. Review events of the last year and see how God has worked in your lives.

Anytime

You can probably think of other times to practice Deuteronomy 6:4-7 in your normal family routine. Be creative! Above all, enjoy time with your family as you nurture Christian faith.

The Great Distraction

Name one invention of the 20th century that has caused families to waste billions of hours. If you answered "television," you are correct. In a day when people say they are busier than ever, they consume hours and hours of television weekly. Kids waste away in their bedrooms watching their own televisions apart from adult supervision. Pornography, drugs, alcohol, foul language, put downs, violence, nudity—all things parents and grandparents would never let in the front door are brought into the home through the TV screen. Why not free up family time by watching television in a deliberate manner? Here are a few tips that can help:

- Create a deliberate plan of action for choosing what you will watch and what you will avoid.
- Choose ahead of time what you will watch rather than channel surf.
- Limit TV viewing to 1 to 2 hours a day.
- Set basic rules, such as no television during meals or until homework is completed.
- Monitor what your children are watching. Although devices like the V-chip are available to filter offensive programs, they are not a substitute for watching with your children.
- Analyze commercials and talk critically about their messages.

A Bible Passage to Remember

We won't keep secret the glorious deeds and the mighty miracles of the LORD. God gave his Law to Jacob's descendants, the people of Israel. And he told our ancestors to teach their children, so that each new generation would know his Law and tell it to the next. Then they would trust God and obey his teachings, without forgetting anything God had done (Ps 78:4-7).

A Thought to Consider

How do you make room for God in your home?

A Question to Ask Yourself

If nurturing the Christian faith in our children were a crime, would there be enough evidence to convict you?

Dialogue Questions for Group Study

Jumpstart a healthy homegrown faith dialogue in your Sunday school class or small group with the following questions. You can also use "A Bible Passage to Remember," "A Thought to Consider," and "A Question to Ask Yourself" at the end of each chapter to spark a lively discussion.

1. Look at the inventory. What is a growth area you would like to strengthen?
2. What surprised you the most about the Top Ten HomeGrown Faith Practices?
3. How could your congregation help you with the Top Ten HomeGrown Faith Practices?
4. Pick a family routine (traveling to soccer practice, bedtime, etc). How could you make nurturing the Christian faith part of that time?
5. How is TV the "great distraction" in your family? What are you willing to do to reduce the amount of time your family wastes in front of the television?

Chapter Three

A Church Your Children Deserve

These are things we learned from our ancestors, and we will tell them to the next generation. We won't keep secret the glorious deeds and the mighty miracles of the LORD (Ps 78:3-4).

The Davis Family

"Mom, have you seen my jacket?" K.C. called from the hall. "You know, my baseball jacket."

"Not since yesterday," Bonnie said. "I saw it sitting on the bench after you finished practice." Bonnie knew exactly which jacket K.C. was talking about. It had the name and logo of his favorite baseball team. He had not let it out of his sight since he got it for his birthday three weeks before.

K.C. walked from room to room poking around looking for the jacket. "You picked it up right? Do you know where you put it when we got home?" He walked into the kitchen.

"K.C., I didn't pick it up." Bonnie looked up from the grocery list she was writing. "I thought you would get it."

K.C. stopped and looked across the kitchen table at his mom. "Mom," he said in an exasperated tone, "you saw it. Why didn't you pick it up?"

"Hey, I'm sorry," she said. "It's your jacket, I thought you would get it."

"Mom!" K.C. wailed, "my jacket!"

"I know sweetie," she gave him a hug, "it's your favorite. Why don't we get in the car and go back to the park and look for it?"

"OK." K.C. shrugged his shoulders. "But I bet someone took it already."

Bonnie stopped as they reached the door. "You know, K.C., I think this would be a good time for us to pray."

"Oh, Mom," K.C. rolled his eyes. "Come on, we need to get to the park."

"No really, K.C.," she said. "This is one of those times when we can ask God for help."

"OK, go ahead."

"Dear Lord," Bonnie prayed. "You know that K.C. would like to find his jacket, and we ask you to help us as we look for it. But if we can't find it, I ask that you be with K.C. because he will be sad. Help him feel your comforting presence. Thank you. Amen."

"OK, let's go." K.C. opened the door and walked toward the car. He was inside and had his seatbelt on before his mom even got her door open. "Hurry up, Mom," he pleaded.

An hour later, after searching nearly the entire park, K.C. and his mom walked through the front door. He plopped down on the sofa, looking very dejected.

"I knew we wouldn't find it," he sighed. "I thought if we prayed it would be there where I left it."

"I know honey, but that must not be what God planned. Remember we also prayed that God would help you with your feelings if you didn't find it and also help you learn from this experience." His mom sat down beside him on the couch.

"I learned to make sure I have all my stuff with me before I leave places," he said.

"That's right, K.C." she said.

"I'm sorry I blamed you, Mom."

"I know," she said, hugging him. "I forgive you!"

The God Building

What does a lost jacket have to do with homegrown faith?

We cannot talk about homegrown faith without talking about the church. It is through the church that God's purposes are worked out in our world. The church is where the action is! It is where faith is formed and nurtured. Unfortunately, we have a distorted picture of the church in the United States today. What comes to mind when you hear the word *church*? For many people, *church* is associated with a building; we "go to" *church*; we worship God at *church*; we learn about Jesus in *church*. Church is considered a place we go to rather than an identity.

"Why does it matter that we view the church as the building?" you may ask. "Why is equating *church* with a building so dangerous?" The unfortunate connection of the word *church* with a building has had unintended negative consequences in America.

Here are three disturbing falsehoods our children are learning when adults equate church with a building.

You go to the church building to get a weekly dose of God.

Relying on trips to a building to seek God's presence teaches our kids that God is trapped in a box. God then needs to be visited in this God Box or God Building. During the week God becomes irrelevant. By adulthood, God becomes irrelevant on Sundays as well.

Our distorted picture of the church is adversely affecting our children and youth. They are catching an anemic faith and erroneous theology. If we want God to be the center of our lives and the lives of our kids, then we must make God relevant everyday. The building becomes irrelevant; the congregation and the home become key to passing on the faith to our children and our grandchildren.

We have heard many empty-nest parents say, "I brought up my children in the church, but they dropped out as adults." The reality for most of these parents is that they raised their children in a church building. Simply taking kids to a building does not ensure they

Parents Matter: Faith Conversations

A look at the research

God wants the home and congregation to partner. Here's one of many research studies that clearly indicates the importance of a homegrown faith supported by a congregation.

Two sets of adults, both raised by parents who went to church with them, were questioned about how their parents passed on the Christian faith. One set of adults reported that, as high school students, their parents never talked about their Christian faith at home with them.

The other set of adults said their parents often talked at home about their faith. The results of these two faith formation strategies are fascinating.

Adults whose parents talked often at home about the Christian faith during their high school years were four times more likely to trust in a personal Christ than those adults who grew up in homes with parents who never talked about faith.

Wow, keep those faith conversations going!

"Early Adolescents and Their Parents," (Minneapolis, MN: Search Institute, 1984).

are participating in the gathered church, the congregation. Surprisingly, in the United States today, a young person can move through a congregation's age-graded programs without spending much time with Christians from other generations. Young people reach the age of 18 having spent most of their time with their peers. They have never been fully integrated into the life of the congregation and their mission in the world. Is it important for children and teenagers to be with others their own age? Yes, but not to the exclusion of interaction with those of other ages. Likewise, it is important for adults to spend time with other adults at the church building.

An estimated 65 to 75 percent of children and teenagers who have participated in congregational ministries abandon them by age 21. Of those, 60 percent will not return by age 35.[13]

The American Religious Identification Survey of 2001 (a random sample survey of 50,000 Americans) uncovered some startling results.[14] The survey compared Americans' religious identification in 2001 with similar data from 1990.

In 1990, 90 percent of American adults identified with a religious group; this dropped to 81 percent by 2001. Eighty-six percent of American adults identified themselves as Christians in 1990; this dropped significantly to 77 percent by 2001. In 1990, 8 percent of all American adults did not identify themselves with any religious group. This increased to 14 percent by 2001. Note that these statistics were not of membership or congregational participation. They would drop dramatically if worship attendance were the measure.

Overall, participation in congregations in the United States is declining. Particular congregations may be adding numbers or have large numbers of children and teenagers attending, but as the data suggests, most of these young people will not be around after age 21.

[13] Roland Martinson, project chairperson of "The Study of Exemplary Congregations in Youth Ministry," reported at the It's a God Thing! Conference, April 2005, Phoenix, AZ.

[14] Barry A. Kosmin, Egon Mayer, and Ariela Keysar, "The American Religious Identification Survey, 2001," (New York: The Graduate Center of the City University of New York, December 2001).

Faith is a personal, private matter.

Kids learn quickly that if they do not learn about God outside the four walls of the church building, then a relationship with God is a hush-hush, private matter. What do you think happens to kids raised with this perspective? A faith that is rarely talked about is rarely practiced. And a faith that is rarely practiced does not grow. In fact, it withers and dies. There is so much grabbing at our kids' attention that encourages them to talk. Television executives want your kids to talk—to spread the word of materialism. The porn pushers want your kids to talk—to spread the words of smut. The drug pushers want your kids to talk—to spread the words of compulsion and addiction. The cult and new age religious leaders want your kids to talk—to spread the words of deception.

Our faith is not a private matter! Our relationship with God must be integrated into everyday family life. We can talk often with our children and teenagers about our faith at home. Interestingly, if we see a good movie we will tell our friends about it; a good movie becomes the discussion point in the lunch room at work or at the gym. How much more should we talk about our faith with our kids?

Faith formation is best left to the paid professionals and their trained volunteers.

Leaving the nurturing of our kids' faith to the experts is one of the most serious parenting and grandparenting mistakes Christians make today. American Christianity has developed a drop-off mentality where children and teenagers are deposited at the church building so that the faith experts can teach them about Jesus and the Christian faith. Parents have two roles—taxi driver and time keeper—get their kids to the church building and pick them up on time. We would be better off if we had the kids stay home and have the parents come to the church building to learn how to pass on the faith. Don't misunderstand. Congregations need a paid and volunteer staff committed to working with children and youth.

Could You Do This?

Joey walked sleepily down the hall. He had just awakened from his nap and was looking for his grandma. As he entered the living room, he saw her sitting in her favorite chair.

"Hi, Grandma," said Joey quietly as he stood by her chair.

"Hi, sweetie." She gave him a kiss on the head. He would never tell this to his brother, but he kind of liked it when Grandma kissed him like that.

"Are you reading your Bible, Grandma?" Joey asked. Usually if Grandma was reading, she was reading her Bible.

"I am." She pulled him onto her lap. "Want to know what story I'm reading?"

"Sure." Joey snuggled closer. His grandma told him some pretty good stories that she read in the Bible. "What is this one about?"

"Well, I was reading about a little boy just like you. He was with a large group of people who were listening to Jesus preach."

"The real Jesus?" asked Joey skeptically. He had heard a few preachers talk about Jesus but he couldn't imagine what it would be like to hear *Him*.

"Yep, the real Jesus," she said. "Anyway, everyone was getting hungry and the only food around was a few fish and some pieces of bread that the little boy had in his basket."

"He brought his own lunch." Joey approved.

"That's right," she said. "But then a miracle happened, and Jesus fed all the people with the few fish and pieces of bread that the boy had in the basket."

"Cool!"

"You're right!" She smiled. "Bible stories are very cool."

Could You Do This?

"Come here, boys." Anna motioned to her grandsons, then sat down at the kitchen table. "I want to show you something." She reached into her purse, and while the boys watched, she slowly fanned out a large number of one-dollar bills.

"Grandma!" Matt's voice was filled with amazement. "That's the most money I have ever seen!"

"You're right, Matt," she said. "It is a lot of money."

Joey reached out to touch the bills. "How much is there?"

"There are one hundred dollar bills here."

"Are you going to buy a car?" asked Joey, still amazed at the amount of money before him.

"No, Joey," said Anna, "there's not quite enough money to buy a car. But there is enough to help some people this Christmas. How would you like to help me spend it?"

"Really?" asked Matt. "What can we buy?"

"Well, the family we are buying things for has three little boys. Two are about your size, and they have a little baby. They need some toys and clothes," she answered.

"Wow," said Joey. "I know some great toys we can buy."

"Well, then we better get going," said Anna. "But before we leave, I think we should ask God to help us make our decisions."

"She means we're supposed to pray," whispered Joey to his brother.

"That's right, Joey." Anna reached for their hands and bowed her head. "Dear Lord, bless the family that we are buying presents for today. Help them feel your love this holiday season. Amen."

"Amen!" Matt shouted. "Toy store, here we come!"

But congregational ministries led by paid and volunteer staff can only *supplement* what is happening in the home. Again, we must remember the "Deuteronomy Promise" and the abundance of research that clearly demonstrates the importance of parental influence on faith and values development. Do not out-source nurturing the faith to paid professionals. Instead, partner with your congregation, doing what you can while at the church building and at home.

A Look at the Church

A church is a gathering of Christians. There is the universal church—a phrase that describes all the Christians around the globe. There are congregations—local meetings of Christians who meet on a regular basis. In Matthew 18:20 Jesus says, *Whenever two or three of you come together in my name, I am there with you.* That is what *church* is about, a community of faith, the family of God, a people gathered in the name of Jesus. In our family, we talk about this as *big church. Big church* describes the faith community we participate in on Sundays, Wednesdays, and other occasions during the week. We gather together with other Christians for worship, fellowship, education, service, prayer, and more. We practice the ways of faith together.

Little church is the domestic church, where two or more family members live out, wrestle with, and test our faith every day. Yes, a family is a faith community. Your family members gathered together in the name of Jesus are a *little church.* A married couple working out their faith together is a picture of a *little church.* A single mom with two kids praying before mealtime is an example of a *little church.* A dad, step-mom, and three teenagers having a faith conversation while driving is a type of *little church.*

Perhaps you are hearing this notion of home as church for the first time. You may be thinking, "Does that mean we no longer need our congregation?" Not at all! If anything, you need your congregation more than ever. For your children to be followers of Christ as adults, both a *big church* and a *little church* are necessary and critically important.

You and your family need to participate in the larger faith community expressed in your congregation. The ministries of your congregation can help your family grow in faith, and your family members can touch the lives of members of your congregation as you live together in mission.

What Does a Church Your Children Deserve Look Like?

Let's take the concepts of the *big church* and the *little church* to build a framework that helps us understand the kind of church you need for your children to be Christ followers as adults. First, let's look at your faith community (see Figure One). The *big church* is your congregation-centered faith community that you and your family participate in with other Christian families of all generations. Your church has a name like First Baptist, Faith Lutheran, Christ Presbyterian, St. Paul's, or Northside Community. Your church meets somewhere, perhaps in a school or in a designated building.

The *little church* is your home-centered faith community called your family. Christ's presence

Parents Matter: The Wrong Crowd

A look at the research

Young people living in a big city are often associated with gangs, drugs, and delinquent behavior. Conventional wisdom maintains parents raising kids in socially disadvantaged urban environments have little, if any, influence on their children. A recent longitudinal study contradicts this thinking. Researchers found that teenagers were much less likely to associate with deviant peers when they were closely supervised by parents throughout childhood. Parents do matter! Monitoring your child's whereabouts is critical.

Jacqueline J. Lloyd and James C. Anthony, "Hanging Out With the Wrong Crowd: How Much Difference Can Parents Make in an Urban Environment?" *Journal of Urban Health: Bulletin of the New York Academy of Medicine*, (80.3 September 1, 2003), 383-399.

in your family makes it a church. Perhaps not everyone living in your home is a Christian, but because Christ is present through you, your family is a church. The early Christian church was both congregation-centered and home-centered. Acts 2:46-47 gives us a clear picture of the partnership between home and congregation: *Day after day they met together in the temple* [congregation-centered]. *They broke bread together in different homes* [home-centered] *and shared their food happily and freely, while praising God. Everyone liked them, and each day the Lord added to their group others who were being saved.*

Congregations today are reclaiming home as church. You are part of a growing trend

Figure One

FAITH COMMUNITY

← →

Home-Centered
Practicing faith in everyday life, individually or with family, to live faithfully.

Congregation-Centered
Practicing faith with God's family to live faithfully.

returning to the biblical tradition practiced in both the Old and New Testament times that nurtured and celebrated the domestic church along with congregational ministry.

There is also a generational focus to the church (see the continuum in Figure Two). Both age-graded and cross-generational aspects of ministry exist in every congregation as well as every Christian home. You are a church at home, and there your kids are learning how to live out the Christian faith practically. In some Christian homes, the ways of faith (prayer, Bible reading, faith conversations, acts of service, and the like) are not practiced and faith is not lived out. Adult children who came from these homes are less likely to follow Christ. Homes where the ways of faith are practiced regularly and living out the Christian faith is talked about, struggled with, and practiced will more likely have adult children who do follow Christ.

Of course, as we have said before, there is no guarantee! But your chances as a parent of seeing your adult children live for Jesus are far greater if you intentionally create a home where your faith is lived out daily. Will you make mistakes? Certainly. Will you struggle? Of course. Will you find that your efforts pay off? Absolutely. God will honor your efforts.

The two continuums, *Faith Community* and *Generational Focus*, represent a reality that is dynamic and fluid. For example, there are all kinds of faith communities from a mother and son to a small group or Sunday school class to a large congregation. This is true as well for the generational focus. A church, including the home, can have from two to five generations represented in any given ministry.

Combine the two continuums (see Figure Three), and you have four windows of ministry activity. All four windows are necessary for parents, grandparents, caring adults, and congregational leaders to pass on the faith successfully to the next generation. There are different ministry activities that occur in each of the four windows.

Window #1: Congregation-Centered, Age-Graded Ministry

This is the ministry area where the *Big Church*, the congregation and its ministries, is at its best in the United States today. Families arrive at the church building and move to their various age-graded ministry experiences—Sunday school, youth worship, adult Bible studies, and more. All these ministries are important and needed. And you, as a parent can get involved in ways that make a difference. It can be easy to fall into the roles of taxi and time keeper (remember, get kids to the program and pick them up on time), leaving the job of faith formation to your congregation's paid staff or other volunteers.

A Word of Caution: Remember the Deuteronomy Promise!

Figure Two

GENERATIONAL FOCUS

← →

Age-Graded

Separating the generations into distinct generational groups to grow in Christ.

Cross†Generational

Gathering the generations together to grow in Christ.

Figure Three

A Church Your Children Deserve

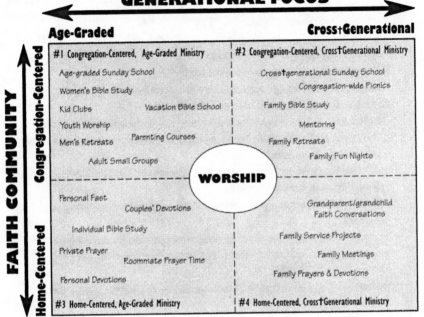

GENERATIONAL FOCUS

Age-Graded		Cross†Generational

FAITH COMMUNITY

Congregation-Centered

#1 Congregation-Centered, Age-Graded Ministry

Age-graded Sunday School

Women's Bible Study

Kid Clubs　　　Vacation Bible School

Youth Worship

Men's Retreats　Parenting Courses

Adult Small Groups

#2 Congregation-Centered, Cross†Generational Ministry

Cross†generational Sunday School

Congregation-wide Picnics

Family Bible Study

Mentoring

Family Retreats

Family Fun Nights

WORSHIP

Home-Centered

Personal Fast

　Couples' Devotions

Individual Bible Study

Private Prayer

　　Roommate Prayer Time

Personal Devotions

Grandparent/grandchild
Faith Conversations

Family Service Projects

Family Meetings

Family Prayers & Devotions

#3 Home-Centered, Age-Graded Ministry | **#4 Home-Centered, Cross†Generational Ministry**

The Deuteronomy Promise

God's wonderful plan for living by faith is best passed on to children, including teenagers, through the home within the normal routines of family life so that kids and their parents (and extended family) can together experience the joy of living in grace as they follow Christ and so that these kids as adults will choose to be Christfollowers.
(See Deuteronomy 6:4-7, 20-25; 11:1-28; 32:46-47.)

Your congregation's age-graded ministries, as good as they may be, can never take the place of homegrown faith. How you work nurturing faith into the normal routines of your family life will affect your children far more than all of the age-graded ministries of any congregation. Get your children participating in one or more of your congregation's age-graded ministries, and involve yourself in one of them with your children. But never forget that what happens in these age-graded ministries can only supplement what you do at home.

Window #2: Congregation-Centered, Cross-Generational Ministry
Your children, including your teenagers, need interaction with people of faith from all generations, particularly in corporate worship. Too often, a congregation's cross-

generational ministries tend to focus on fellowship. There is nothing wrong with fellowship, but you and your kids need the experience and perspective from people of all ages in your congregation. This is why corporate worship was promoted so vigorously in chapter two. The congregation we attend has limited cross-generational ministry opportunities. We have chosen to develop our own opportunities creatively. Here are a few ideas that we and friends of ours have tried:

- Intentionally find adults who love kids to talk with your children before and after your congregation's worship service.
- Take your teenager with you to a Bible study.
- Take advantage of family-centered activities like retreats and camps.
- Volunteer to teach your child's Sunday school class.
- Find an adult mentor from your congregation to spend time with your child.
- Invite three families to your home for dinner. Plan a short devotional activity during your time together.
- Do a family service project such as raking leaves or cleaning the home of an elderly person in your congregation.
- Advocate for more cross-generational ministry opportunities within your congregation.
- Participate in a play group for your little one with moms and dads from your congregation. Include faith-growing activities in your time together.
- Start a family Bible study.
- Encourage your children's and youth ministry teams to plan cross-generational ministry opportunities.
- Invite other generations to any age-graded program in which you are involved.
- Get more adults involved in your congregation's Vacation Bible School program.
- Involve yourselves in service projects your congregation sponsors.
- Help in the kitchen with your kids at your congregation's next fellowship event.
- Visit one of your congregation's shut-ins.
- Start a cross-generational ministry team within your congregation.

Window #3: Home-Centered, Age-Graded Ministry

Visit your local Christian bookstore, talk with your pastor, seek out a Christian friend whom you admire, and ask them for names of resources to help you grow closer to God. You will not know how important your role modeling has been with your children until you watch how they raise your grandchildren. Also, search the Scriptures for examples of those who spent time in prayer, made personal devotions a priority, fasted, and spent time studying God's Word.

Window #4: Home-Centered, Cross-Generational Ministry

One thing we already know from Scripture and research is that nurturing faith in children and teenagers is not something we can out-source to paid professionals within our congregation. Parents are the number one influencer of faith and values in children and teenagers. We often get some of the following questions at our workshops. We thought they might prove helpful and motivational to read before we launch into planning how you can most easily and effectively do this thing we call homegrown faith.

Question: Isn't the spiritual development of young people the responsibility of the congregation?

Answer: Of course it is. The congregation is in a unique position to help our young people grow in their Christian faith. We know the congregation is doing the best it can in training young people.

Take pastors, for instance. They are preaching from the pulpit, teaching classes, leading Bible studies, and praying for our children. Yet even with their theological training, pastors can only do so much for the spiritual development of young people.

Volunteer children's workers, youth workers, choir and music leaders, and other congregational volunteers are working hard to teach Sunday school or plan retreats. We know they can only do so much. As much as the congregation wants young people to know God and experience the reality of God working in their lives, the congregation cannot do it all.

The answer is partnership. The congregation and the home together can nurture young people in the Christian faith. The congregation and the home, working in partnership, can keep families together and sustain them in a world that seems to be tearing them apart.

Question: What if I don't feel qualified to help my child grow spiritually?

Answer: When it comes to growing the faith of your family, the only qualification is a willing heart. If you want to help your child grow spiritually, then you're qualified; you don't need formal theological training. In fact, you do not even need to know what the word "theological" means. All you need is a passion to see your children grow closer to God. If you have a theological question, remember that you have partnered with your local congregation. Seek counsel from one of your pastors or church leaders.

Question: What if I'm struggling with my own faith?

Answer: Does God feel far away? Do you wish you had more answers? You are in good company. Faithful people from the Bible, such as Abraham, Job, David, and Thomas all felt either alienated from or abandoned by God at times. They were godly individuals, but they all felt sufficiently distanced from God to do some serious doubting. (See Genesis 17:17-22; Job 23:1-17; Psalm 55; Matthew 20:24-29 for their stories.) Few Bible heroes and heroines did not struggle with their faith. So understand the first principle of Christian maturity: Seldom is there spiritual growth without inner struggles, doubts, confusion, or feelings of abandonment.

What if you are in such a season right now and do not have the cheerful clarity you think is necessary to nurture someone else's faith? First, give your doubts, alienation, disappointments, or anger to God. He is big enough to handle them. And whether or not you feel like God is listening, God is.

Second, recognize that God never intended for us to slog our way through doubt and confusion alone. We need support, we need others, and your congregation can be a prime support for you during a dark season. Your connection with God's people can help you in your struggle. Stay connected! Don't try to do this alone.

We grow best in our relationship with God (even when He seems silent) when we do it in community. The congregation is one such community, and your family is another.

If you are currently struggling with your own faith, try this experiment: select one or two of the "Fifty Nifty" activities (chapters seven through twelve) to do with your family. Ask for God's guidance, or ask another family member to pray. See how God works in your family. Do not neglect the nurture of your family's faith because you are feeling down about your own. In fact, your candidness about your own struggle is as important for your family to know about as any fervent Bible lesson you could teach.

Question: What if I still feel uncomfortable about nurturing faith in my children?

Answer: Getting out of your comfort zone will help you grow and develop as a Christian. The discomfort you feel is very common among parents who want to take an active role in the spiritual development of their children. Whether you feel scared, guilty, or overwhelmed, you are not alone. Take a calculated risk. Feel uncomfortable and move forward with several activities during the next month. See how God works in your life and the lives of your family members.

Question: What if my kids aren't interested?

Answer: Tots to teens want to know more about God. They are full of questions about faith, Bible stories, the meaning of life, and the reality of God. They do not want to be bored; they do not even want to be entertained. They want meaningful interaction with you.

So choose activities *with* your kids. Ask them to take a leadership role in doing the activities.

Question: What if I make mistakes?

Answer: If your kids do not see you making mistakes, they might think they have to live mistake-free lives, and you know how disastrous that can be. Of course you will try, fail, make mistakes, and suffer setbacks. You will also have fun together, build up each other's faith, create very meaningful memories, and grow closer to each other and to God.

Question: What if I can't answer my child's questions about God or faith?

Answer: Tell them the truth. Say, "I don't know." Then look up the answer together in the Bible, a reference book, the Internet, or other reliable sources.

Your pastor can be a great resource for direction. Ask someone whom you trust and respect who has already raised children your kids' ages. On the other hand, some questions do not need to be or cannot be answered now, and that's OK.

Doing Church Differently

You are reading this book because you want your kids to be people of faith as adults. You want them to follow Christ from four years old to 40 years old. You want your children as adults to participate actively in the life of a congregation and its mission. You cannot achieve this goal alone; your family needs a congregation. But neither do you want to neglect homegrown faith. Leaving the task of passing on the Christian faith to a congregation alone often ends in disaster. Growing up Christian takes both a *big church* and a *little church*.

We began this chapter with the story of the lost jacket, a story of how the domestic church, the *little church*, nurtures the Christian faith. In this story, a young boy learns from his mother that God is with him even in the bad times. His mom became the bearer of this message. You are the minister in your *little church* called home. May God bless you as you minister!

A Bible Passage to Remember

Day after day they met together in the temple. They broke bread together in different homes and shared their food happily and freely, while praising God. Everyone liked them, and each day the Lord added to their group others who were being saved (Ac 2:46-47).

A Thought to Consider

Passing on faith to your children and teenagers requires a balanced ministry, one that includes four ministry windows: age-graded, cross-generational, home-centered, and congregation-centered.

A Question to Ask Yourself

How is your family involved in all four ministry windows?

Dialogue Questions for Group Study

Jumpstart a healthy homegrown faith dialogue in your Sunday school class or small group with the following questions. You can also use "A Bible Passage to Remember," "A Thought to Consider," and "A Question to Ask Yourself" at the end of each chapter to spark a lively discussion.

1. How reliant are you on those ministry activities that occur in the *big church* to teach faith to your children?
2. How is your family a faith community (the *little church*)?
3. What kinds of things could you as a parent do to involve your kids in more cross-generational experiences within your congregation?
4. What would you be willing to do differently to grow closer to God?
5. How could you partner creatively with your congregation to do a better job at homegrown faith?

Chapter Four

The Future Does Not Arrive Unannounced

Tell our children! Let it be told to our grandchildren and their children too (Joel 1:3).

40 Years in the Future

The Davis Family

"I can't believe she's gone," Jenna said as they stood waiting for the service to begin. Jenna stood with her brothers Chris and K.C. in the small chapel of the congregation they had attended with their mother so many years ago.

The service brought back memories for the three siblings. The minister spoke fondly of their mother, Bonnie, who was one of the oldest members of the congregation. Their father was never really involved with the congregation, but Bonnie made sure they went with her to worship, Sunday school, VBS, and more. She taught several of their Sunday school classes and enjoyed volunteering with the youth group.

Her faith did not stop at the church building either.

"Do you remember how we would pray every time we got into the car with Mom? She still did it with my kids!" Chris whispered to his sister, "I'm doing it now too!"

"I always remember her talking to us enthusiastically about what we learned in Sunday school," said K.C. "I never really thought about all the time she spent on things like that. She always seemed to find a way to help us grow spiritually. It started out with little things like reading Bible stories to us at night or praying before meals. And then when we were older and she had to drive us places, we would end up getting into these discussions about how God would want us to handle situations in our lives."

"Yeah, she always would ask me what I thought Jesus would do whenever I had a problem or a tough question to answer." Jenna wiped her eyes.

The service was beautiful. Bonnie's children were surprised to learn how many other lives their mother had influenced for the Lord. A man shared how Bonnie would write him letters of encouragement and promise to keep him in her prayers while he was away from home in the Army. A woman shared how Bonnie had helped her take care of her children when she was sick.

At the gathering after the funeral, an older woman approached Jenna, K.C., and

Chris. "Excuse me," she whispered. "I don't want to bother you at a time like this, but I wanted you to know how much your mom meant to my family."

The brothers and sister nodded to each other in puzzlement.

"My name is Claire Simms. I'm not even sure if your mom really knew me, but I watched how involved she was with you three. I saw how she came to church with you and tried to encourage your love for the Lord. I just want you to know that I tried to be like her with my children. My son's a minister now, and my daughter is passing on the faith to her children. It probably wouldn't have happened without your mother's influence."

"Why...thank you, Mrs. Simms. My mother would have appreciated knowing how well your family is doing."

More people stopped and talked to Bonnie's children as the afternoon progressed. They got a very clear picture of her affect on not just them, but on the many other people she knew.

The Collins Family

It's a typical Saturday and the Collins family is busy planning the one day of the week that their family can spend time together, Sunday. Tomorrow is a big day because Dan Collins' brother Louie and his sister Carla and their families are coming to spend the day. There is a lot of work to be done before the families arrive.

"What time will they get here?" asked Joy, Beth and Dan's youngest daughter. It was always fun when her cousins came over.

"Everyone is supposed to get here by 10:00," Beth answered.

"Dad, can we play a while before we eat lunch tomorrow?" Danny, Joy's younger brother, walked into the room. "I want to show Cousin Josh what I got for my birthday."

"If everyone gets here at 10:00 like we planned, there will be time for you to play," said his father.

"Dad, my friend Tina goes to church on Sunday with her parents. She couldn't believe it when I told her that we never go to church," Joy blurted out. She quietly added, "Why don't we ever go to church?"

Dan considered this. "I remember my parents taking me to church for awhile when I was a kid. They thought it would be good for us, so we went every Sunday. Mom even had us listening to Christian radio stations in the car. But then we missed a Sunday here and there and pretty soon we were doing other things like errands or sports on Sunday. Sometimes we were tired, so we just wanted to sleep in. I don't think my brother and sister take their families to church much anymore either. If they did, we couldn't be doing things like we are doing tomorrow, could we?"

"I was sent to Sunday school when I was a kid," Beth remembered. "But my parents never seemed interested in doing the church thing together."

"But why don't we go to church?" Joy persisted.

"We do go to church, Joy," said her mom, "on Christmas and Easter. I think it's important for a family to go then, but if you want to try it more we could take you sometime. Couldn't we, Dan?"

"Sure. We could drop you off, run a few errands, and be back in time to pick you up. We'll talk about it later Joy, I promise," Dan changed the subject, "but right now we need to get ready for tomorrow."

The Goodman Family

Leah was taking a walk with her father.

"My little girl is going to be a mommy. I can't wait to spoil the kid rotten and send him home to you!" her father Matt said, giving her shoulder a squeeze.

"If *she* gets too spoiled, I'm sending her to live with you!" laughed Leah. "But really, Dad, I hope you and Mom will be involved. This parenting thing sounds like an awfully big job, and Jeff and I want to do it right."

"It is," said Matt, "and I hope I can be there for my grandchild like my grandma was for me and your uncle."

"Great-grandma Anna really meant a lot to you and Uncle Joey, didn't she? You talk so much about her, I almost feel as if I know her. I wish I could have," Leah sighed.

"You would have liked her Leah, and I'm not sure I would be the person I am today without her," said Matt. "My parents were so busy with work that Grandma Anna practically raised us. It sounds silly now I know, but I felt Grandma Anna had this special relationship with God. She always made it sound like she had just spoken to God. She probably did because she prayed all the time."

"I remember you saying that she told you she thought God was keeping her alive to pray for you and Uncle Joey. I bet that made you think twice about doing anything wrong," laughed Leah.

"That's for sure!"

Leah grew very quiet. "I know I always thought about you and Mom praying for me," she said. "It kept me out of a lot of trouble."

"I'm glad to hear it, I think. But it wasn't just praying. Grandma Anna was the one who made sure church and God were real to us. We knew our parents believed in God, and they made sure we went to church, but somehow Grandma Anna made it feel such a part of our lives. She prayed, not just *for* us, but *with* us so that we knew how to pray and felt comfortable with it. She would play Christian music until we knew all the words as well as she did. All the Bible stories and verses that I know are because Grandma Anna encouraged me to learn them. And if we were in church, she was in church, either sitting with us in the service or helping out in our classes or groups. I don't know how she had the energy."

"She must have really loved you," Leah said.

"She did, and she really loved God and wanted that relationship for us, too," said Matt. "I hope I can share that with my grandson."

"Grand*daughter*!" Leah corrected him. She whispered, "I hope so, too."

Three Families

Here we have three families, each with stories to tell of a relationship with God. Jenna, Chris, and K.C.—all Christfollowers as adults. Their mother, Bonnie, knew the three of them would love the Lord 40 years in the future because she raised them to follow Christ.

The Collinses are an extended family committed to family life but not to God. You could have predicted their situation. They were raised to leave God out of their family life, except of course, on Christmas and Easter.

Leah Goodman is passionate about raising her child to love God. What a legacy her great-grandmother Anna left. Leah's faith was shaped by her great-grandmother long before she was even born!

Millions of family faith stories around the world are taking place right now. Only three have been told here. Each family has their own story of faith in something or someone. What is your story? Are you ready to write new chapters in that faith story?

The future does not arrive unannounced! You can know how the story ends for your children 40 years from now. You can predict with confidence the spiritual choices your children will make as adults. You can influence what your children will do with God in their adult lives. You can create the home conditions under which faith in Jesus Christ is nurtured in your kids.

How can you know your children's spiritual future will not arrive unannounced? Is it guaranteed that if you apply the principles given in this book, your children will be Christfollowers as adults?

There is no money-back guarantee. God gives each of us the choice to have or not to have a relationship with Jesus Christ. God does not hold parents responsible for the choices of their children anymore than He holds children responsible for the choices of their parents. Parents are not to be blamed if their children do not choose to follow Christ as adults.[15]

With that said, we also must recognize that it is in our power as parents to heighten

Could You Do This?

Bonnie spread the blanket out on a shady patch of grass near the lake. She had brought her children out for a picnic to celebrate their "half-birthdays," a holiday that she had made up when her kids were small. All of their birthdays fell during the same month, and there was such a long time between one birthday and the next. The whole family used to celebrate together, but this year her husband Frank needed to work, so Bonnie decided to bring them out to the lake anyway.

"Put the basket over there," she told her son Chris. "Jenna, you can start to take things out. K.C., please put the juice down by Jenna."

The children carefully put the items down on the blanket, and Bonnie started to put their food on their plates.

"Here you go." She handed them their plates. "Let's pray before we eat." One thing Bonnie made sure that the kids did was thank God for the food they received. They always took time to pray before each meal, even when they were out. They bowed their heads. "Thank you, Lord, for this food and for another year together. Amen."

After the children finished eating, they went to play on the playground near the lake. Bonnie enjoyed watching them. "They're growing up so fast, Lord," she whispered. "Please keep them safe."

When the children returned to help their mother clean up, she asked them to sit down for a few moments. "I just wanted to tell you how much I love you, and how thankful I am that God gave you to your father and me. I am very proud of you."

There was a brief silence before Chris said, "We love you, too, Mom." After hugging each other, they began to pack up their things for the trip home.

---

[15] De 24:16, Job 19:4, Je 31:30, Ez 18:20.

the likelihood that our kids will be Christfollowers as adults. There are certain conditions that we can create in our homes and in our congregations that leave a legacy of faith for our children, grandchildren, and beyond. We can pass on the faith to our children and trust that God will honor our efforts.

How Do We Know Our Kids Will Be Christfollowers as Adults?

Let's begin to answer this question by examining one small but significant passage found in the Old Testament. The passage is Proverbs 22:6. This verse could be paraphrased, *Walk and talk Jesus at home with your children today and when they are grown they will walk and talk Jesus.* Wow, what a hopeful promise.

Consider what God is telling you. Your sons and your daughters will one day follow Jesus if you strive to follow Him today. In between adolescence and adulthood, your kids may or may not follow Jesus, but rest assured, how you parent today will pay off in the future. Whatever you walk and talk today will be what your children walk and talk tomorrow!

Unfortunately, the opposite is also true.[16] If parents do not walk with and talk about Jesus at home, it is likely their kids will not be Christfollowers as adults. Whatever is walked and talked by parents will be reflected in their children.

*Train up a child in the way he should go: and when he is old, he will **not depart** from it (Pr 22:6, KJV).*

The words *not depart* are printed in bold to make a point. The passage does not say train your children in the faith, and every minute of every day they will follow Jesus. It does, however, clearly point to the end result. Adult children who caught faith at home while growing up will most likely live out that faith as adults. They may live every year of their adult lives for Jesus. Or they may depart from the faith for a season. It may take bumping into the realities of our fallen, sinful world and their own brokenness to get

---

[16] Some teenagers whose parents are not Christians react to their parents' agnostic views or hedonistic practices and discover God and His ways apart from their parents. But the norm is that children respond to their upbringing. Teenagers intentionally raised at home to be atheists tend to be atheists and vice versa.

them to return. The storms of life we all inevitably face have a way of bringing adult children back to the faith of their childhood.

God does not require that any parent be successful, only faithful. It is not difficult. Turn over to Christ all of your parenting efforts. He is waiting each day for you to *leave all your worries with him, because he cares for you (1 Pe 5:7, GNB)*. God is not expecting you to do this on your own. He wants to pass on the Christian faith to your children through you. Faith growing with your children is something God will do working *through you* if you surrender to Him!

Passing on the faith to our kids is not about perfection or even perfect parenting! No matter where you are in your own spiritual journey with Christ, no matter how much you know about the Bible, no matter how sinful your past, no matter how busy your schedule, you can grow your kids in the Christian faith. You can have kids that, as grown-ups, are Christ followers. *God can do anything, you know—far more than you could ever imagine or guess or request in your wildest dreams! (Ep 3:20, THE MESSAGE)*.

Your kids as adults may not do "Christianity" exactly as you do. They may not do "church" exactly as you do. But they will "do Jesus" if you walk and talk with Jesus today.

The life experiences of Christians around the world validate the promise God makes to us in Proverbs 22:6. You only need to ask Christians in their senior years if their adult children are Christfollowers, and you will hear how faith was sparked and energized at home and supported at church. The home efforts of these senior citizen saints paid off eventually. Many will have stories of adult kids who strayed from the faith for a time. But their adult children found their way back to the Lord because of a homegrown faith foundation.

Not only is the promise of Proverbs 22:6 validated by life experience, but it also is backed by 30-plus years of social science research. The influence parents have on the faith and values of their children is well documented as we have already mentioned. This research indicates a strong, positive connection between what is walked and talked by parents at home during adolescence and what is walked and talked by their children as adults!

Figure One: Train Up a Child

*Train up a child in the way he should go: and when he is old, he will **not depart** from it (Pr 22:6, KJV)*.

Life Stage	Age	Faith/Values	Actions	Departure
Childhood	Birth-8	_____		Minimal
Preadolescence	9-12	____ ____ ____ ____		Toward Maximum
Adolescence	13-18	___ ___ ___ ___ ___ ___		Maximum
Emerging Adult	19-25	____ ____ ____ ____		Toward Minimal
Adulthood	25+	_____		Minimal

Could You Do This?

"Whoa, guys! We forgot something." Joe stopped on the way out the front door of his mom's house and turned to look at his boys.

"Oh, yeah," said Matt, his oldest son. He motioned for Joe's mom, Anna, to come closer. "We forgot to pray. Grandma, Joey, come on, we need to pray before Dad goes to work."

Anna and Joey came down the hall and met them at the front door.

"Well," said Anna, "we can't miss praying with your dad."

Smiling at his mom, Joe grabbed Joey and Matt's hands. They held onto their grandma's hands. "Dear Lord," Joe said. "Watch over us today. Help us act the way you would want us to and keep us safe."

All four of them said, "Amen."

Joe hugged his sons and his mom and left for work.

Joey watched his dad drive away. "I'm glad we pray with Daddy before he goes."

"Why's that?" Anna asked.

"Because it feels like God is going to take care of him when we do," said Joey.

"Then that's a very good reason for us to pray," said Anna.

In Figure One we have interpreted and distilled our take on this encouraging research. Let's take a look at each of the stages of life found in Figure One and the picture research gives us as each relates to Proverbs 22:6.

Childhood

The first eight years of life find the faith and values of children to be fairly consistent with that of their parents. They catch this faith and system of values from watching their parents' actions, listening to their parents, and living within the boundaries set by their parents. Children, birth to eight, don't significantly *depart* from how they are *trained*. The unbroken line from "Faith/Values" to "Actions" in Figure One represents the consistency found between how kids have been parented (their faith and values) and how they behave (their actions). This applies to positive as well as negative behavior. Kids are trained to be truthful or dishonest, compassionate or cruel, believers or unbelievers.

Preadolescence

The "tween years," or preadolescence, worry parents about how they are raising their children. An inconsistency between the parents' faith and values and children's actions (represented in Figure One by the broken line) emerges. Kids still hold to the faith and values caught from their parents, but it does not always look like they do because of the *departure* from how they were *trained*.

Parents of preadolescents often lay awake at night wondering why their kid decided to try that cigarette, tell that lie, cheat on that homework assignment, steal that piece of candy, act up that way in class, have that attitude about going to worship service, etc. Parents might say, "I never taught him to act like that!"

Adolescence

Raising teenagers often bewilders parents as well as grandparents. Here is a quote that summarizes the thoughts and feelings of many adults in the 21st century. Socrates, a Greek philosopher in Athens from 469 BC to 399 BC, expressed his frustrations with teenagers millennia ago:

"The children now love luxury; they have bad manners, contempt for authority; they show disrespect for elders and love chatter in place of exercise. Children are now tyrants, not the servants of their households. They no longer rise when elders enter the room. They contradict their parents, chatter before company, gobble up dainties at the table, cross their legs, and tyrannize their teachers."

The teen years can be spiritually confusing to parents because this is the life stage when the greatest inconsistency between young people's actions and their faith and values manifest. It is during the teen years that kids question their faith and values the most. The dotted line in Figure One represents this maximum *departure*.

Some teens show little departure from their parents' faith and values. These teens walk and talk Jesus as if doing so was as natural as breathing. It looks so easy for the parents of these kids. Other teens, with a mom, dad, or grandparent who did walk and talk Jesus at home just like the parents who made it look so easy, have teens who seem to be walking away from Jesus. Although some of their actions have departed from their faith and values, this departure will most likely not be permanent. Parents of these kids can stand on the hopeful promise of Proverbs 22:6, documented by research.

Parents Matter: Family

A look at the research

A recent survey reported that teenagers and young adults (born between 1980 and 2000) who grew up in homes in which "religion played an important role" had better relationships with their parents. The survey reports that "family clearly shapes a young person's entry into adulthood...their families nurture them, fundamentally shape them, and teach them their values and how they will connect to community."

Parents who integrate their Christianity into the everyday lives and routines of their families will have a better relationship with their children as those children move into adulthood than parents who keep their faith in the church building. Keep homegrowing your kids' faith!

Anna Greenberg, "OMG! How Generation Y Is Redefining Faith in The iPod Era," www.rebooters.net, 2005.

While rebellion has always existed during the adolescent years, it is not normal. The research of Lawrence Steinberg and others has shown that the "generation gap" is a myth. The majority of teenagers move through their adolescent years feeling close to their parents without serious parent-teen relationship problems. Rebellion during the teen years should signal a red flag for parents. Unfortunately, the conventional wisdom and pop psychology of our day tells parents that rebellion is normal; it is not. If you have had or are having serious problems with your teenager, seek assistance from your pastor, youth pastor, a counselor, or trusted friend. Look for adults in your church whose children have passed through adolescence successfully and glean from their experiences.

Emerging Adult

In bed Sunday mornings, sparse prayer life, planning for the future, sporadically participating in a mid-week Bible study, talking until 3:00 a.m. at a coffee shop about the meaning of life. These behaviors describe young people in their post-high school years. Their spiritual situation can look confusing to parents. Young adults, between 19 and 25 years old, are much like preadolescents. There is more consistency between their actions and the faith and values they caught while growing up. But parents can easily be fooled, just like in the preadolescent years. Keep praying for them. They are learning to integrate their behaviors with their faith and values. They are growing up spiritually.

Adulthood

This is when adult children begin to live more consistently with how they were raised. If their parents walked and talked Jesus, they are now doing the same. Some adult children take longer than others. Although there is no guarantee, normally they are living out the spiritual legacy left them by their parents and grandparents.

Your Job: Point Them in the Jesus Direction

Point your kids in the right direction—when they're old they won't be lost (Pr 22:6, THE MESSAGE).

What a hope for parents with young children! Get them started in the right direction, and as adults they will experience the presence of God in their lives.

What a hope for parents with teenagers! Do your best to keep them on the right path in the right direction. Do this in the midst of their mood swings, as they assert themselves and strive for independence, and when they are grown they will act more like you than you ever imagined.

What a hope for parents of youth and adults not now following Christ! Keep praying for your children. As they face the hardships and crises that life will throw at them, they will return to the faith they caught at home.

This is the hope in Proverbs 22:6. How you walk and talk Jesus *does* matter at every stage of your kids' lives. Your children's future will not arrive unannounced. You can live with the hope that what you do with Jesus at home will make a difference. The conditions you create at home will dramatically shape the spiritual choices your kids make when they are older. Are you ready to walk and talk Jesus with your kids in childhood? During preadolescence? Through adolescence? Into the teenage years? And into adulthood?

A Bible Passage to Remember

I miss you a lot, especially when I remember that last tearful good-bye, and I look forward to a joy-packed reunion. That precious memory triggers another: your honest faith—and what a rich faith it is, handed down from your grandmother Lois to your mother Eunice, and now to you! (2 Ti 1:4-5, THE MESSAGE).

A Thought to Consider

You are the most influential person of faith in your children's lives—more influential than school teachers, coaches, Sunday school teachers, youth workers, or pastors!

A Question to Ask Yourself

Are you willing to do whatever it takes to pass on the Christian faith to your children?

Dialogue Questions for Group Study

Jumpstart a healthy homegrown faith dialogue in your Sunday school class or small group with the following questions. You can also use "A Bible Passage to Remember," "A Thought to Consider," and "A Question to Ask Yourself" at the end of each chapter to spark a lively discussion.

1. How will you as a parent be remembered at your funeral?
2. What kind of faith legacy do you want to leave your great-grandchildren?
3. Can you tell a story of a mom, dad, or grandparent who is raising or has raised their kids to be Christ followers?
4. What did you find encouraging about the "Train Up a Child" model?
5. What friend needs the hope communicated in Proverbs 22:6? How can you encourage this friend?

Chapter Five

The Joshua Question

And let it be a warning that you must teach your children to obey everything written in The Book of God's Law. The Law isn't empty words. It can give you a long life in the land that you are going to take (De 32:46-47).

The Davis Family

It's a typical Saturday at the Davis house. Once again Bonnie is trying to get her husband interested in going to church the next day with her and the kids.

"No, Bonnie, we already talked about this a million times. I'm not going to church with you on Sunday." Frank turned on the television.

"But you haven't gone with us the last three Sundays, Frank. It doesn't set a good example for the kids."

"Look Bonnie," Frank barked, "you know that the play-offs for my softball team are this Sunday. It's important that I be there. That teaches the kids that their dad keeps his commitments. Besides, you go to church enough for the both of us."

"Ok, so Sunday is out. How about coming to the worship service on Saturday night with us?" she said hopefully. "It's more upbeat so you would probably like it. Maybe we could go out to dinner afterwards and have fun together."

"I work hard all week, and I don't ask for much. The only time I get to relax is on the weekend. There's a game on TV that I want to watch. Besides, going to church on a Saturday night is not exactly my idea of a way to relax." He flipped through the channels. "But I do like the going out to dinner part. I could meet you at the restaurant after church. That way we could still go out together as a family and have some fun."

"Sure," Bonnie sighed, "I'll just go with the kids on Saturday night."

"Great, I'm glad we settled that." Frank found the game on TV. "Hey, Chris, the game's on," he called to his son.

As Bonnie turned and walked out of the room, she said a silent prayer. "Lord, help me. I want my kids to know more about you. Show me the way to make spiritual things a part of their lives. Help Frank to understand that learning more about you is important to our family."

The Collins Family

Liz and Sam Collins waved at their kids as they dropped them off at the door of children's church.

"You know the kids seem to really like it in there." Liz returned to the car with Sam. "Yeah, they are always talking about the Bible stories and singing the little songs they have learned," said Sam.

"Don't I know it." Liz rolled her eyes. "That Christian music CD Carla won in children's church is all we listen to in the car now. Even *I* know most of the words!"

As they sat together drinking coffee, Liz pointed to the information a Sunday school teacher had given her. "Wow, look at all these activities for the kids!"

Sam nodded at the first few choices but then he began to shake his head.

"Liz," he said, "we can't get the kids to all that stuff. Dan is starting baseball in two weeks, and Carla will be having swim meets. Louie won't want to go to church by himself. We need to sit down and prioritize our weekend time."

Driving back to pick up their kids, Sam noticed that his wife was looking out the window of the car. "Hey, where are you?" he asked.

"Oh, sorry, I was just thinking about what a beautiful day it is and how it's a shame that the kids have to spend it inside," Liz sighed.

"I know what you mean." Sam looked out the door window. "Maybe next Sunday we could go on a hike with the kids and have a picnic. You know, spend some quality time together. It seems like when they go to church we never have a chance to be together. The kids go one direction and we go another."

Liz sighed. "We get so busy that some Sunday mornings I would just like to stay in bed and relax and read the paper. Sometimes it seems like we need a weekend to recover from our weekend!"

The Goodman Family

"You have to start working on Sundays, too!" Sandy said, exasperated. "How are we going to get the boys to church with both of us working? They have really started to enjoy their Sunday school classes, and I would hate for them to miss it."

"I know." Joe smiled. "They talk a mile a minute when they get home about what they learned about the Bible. I'm really glad they are learning that stuff. But I just don't know how we can do it now."

"I was hoping we could both start helping out in their classes, but if we are both working that's out of the question. I guess they're just going to miss out," his wife sighed. "Especially now that it looks like this could be a permanent thing for both of us."

Joe and Sandy worked hard at being good parents. As Christians, they had decided that when the time came for them to have kids they would make sure their kids actively participated in church. They just hadn't counted on Joe losing his old job and Sandy having to work. Things were tight, and Joe was now working two jobs. They had always tried to juggle their work schedules so their kids wouldn't miss out on things they enjoyed.

"Wait a minute!" Joe remembered. "What about my mom? She loves it that we are taking the kids to church. Maybe if we explained the situation to her she wouldn't mind taking them on the Sundays when we are working. I know she always made sure my brother and I went."

"That's a great idea! She's always asking them what they have learned or reading them a story in her big Bible. She seems kind of lost since your dad died. I bet she would do it! Let's invite her over for dinner, and we can ask her then."

After dinner that night, Joe asked his mom Anna the big question, "Mom, Sandy and I both have to start working more hours. Both of us will be working on Sunday mornings from now on. Would you mind taking the kids to Sunday school and worship on Sunday mornings?"

After this rush of words was silence. Joe and Sandy nervously looked at each other.

"Mom," Joe backpedaled, "It's OK if you can't. I know it would mean going to a different service, but…" Joe stopped talking when he saw his mom smile.

"Joe, how could I say no to a question like that? Of course, I'll take the kids. It will be a lot of fun. Do you think I could help in their classes sometimes? I always wanted to do that, but I never had the chance when you and your brother were little."

"I don't think that will be a problem, Mom." Sandy gave her a big hug. "They would love it, and I'm sure their teachers would enjoy the help."

"Let's go tell the kids." Anna looked happier than she had in a long time.

Answering the Joshua Question

These are three different families with parents answering the "Joshua Question" differently. Every parent answers the "Joshua Question" every day of the week whether or not they are conscious of it.

What is the Joshua Question? Let's consider it in context. Moses, who led the people of Israel out of Egypt and through the wilderness for 40 years, has died. Joshua is now their leader. He has gathered the leaders of the people for a sermon. The first part of the sermon is a reminder of all the unbelievably great things God has done for the people of Israel even though they did not deserve God's merciful kindness.

> Joshua called the tribes of Israel together for a meeting at Shechem. He had the leaders, including the old men, the judges, and the officials, come up and stand near the sacred tent.
>
> Then Joshua told everyone to listen to this message from the LORD, the God of Israel: Long ago your ancestors lived on the other side of the Euphrates River, and they worshiped other gods. This continued until the time of your ancestor Terah and his two sons, Abraham and Nahor. But I brought Abraham across the Euphrates River and led him through the land of Canaan. I blessed him by giving him Isaac, the first in a line of many descendants.
>
> Then I gave Isaac two sons, Jacob and Esau. I had Esau live in the hill country of Mount Seir, but your ancestor Jacob and his children went to live in Egypt.
>
> Later I sent Moses and his brother Aaron to help your people, and I made all those horrible things happen to the Egyptians. I brought your ancestors out of

Egypt, but the Egyptians got in their chariots and on their horses and chased your ancestors, catching up with them at the Red Sea. Your people cried to me for help, so I put a dark cloud between them and the Egyptians. Then I opened up the sea and let your people walk across on dry ground. But when the Egyptians tried to follow, I commanded the sea to swallow them, and they drowned while you watched. You lived in the desert for a long time, then I brought you into the land east of the Jordan River. The Amorites were living there, and they fought you. But with my help, you defeated them, wiped them out, and took their land. King Balak decided that his nation Moab would go to war against you, so he asked Balaam to come and put a curse on you. But I wouldn't listen to Balaam, and I rescued you by making him bless you instead of curse you. You crossed the Jordan River and came to Jericho. The rulers of Jericho fought you, and so did the Amorites, the Perizzites, the Canaanites, the Hittites, the Girgashites, the Hivites, and the Jebusites. I helped you defeat them all. Your enemies ran from you, but not because you had swords and bows and arrows. I made your enemies panic and run away, as I had done with the two Amorite kings east of the Jordan River.

You didn't have to work for this land—I gave it to you. Now you live in towns you didn't build, and you eat grapes and olives from vineyards and trees you didn't plant (Jos 24:1-13).

Launching into the second half of his sermon, Joshua implores the leaders of the people to act out of gratitude toward God's goodness by obeying and serving Him so this goodness will continue. Since God gives us free will to choose or not choose to serve and worship Him, Joshua gives the people the same choice. They can serve the false gods of the surrounding cultures or they can serve the one true God and continue to receive God's mercy and goodness. God wanted the people of Israel to serve out of a willing heart. He wants the same from us today. This is difficult because the choice is counter to the culture in which we live. Our materialistic culture tries to mold us into serving the gods of materialism, pleasure, power, and prestige. A deliberate choice must be made daily to reject these gods for the God of the Bible.

Then Joshua told the people: Worship the LORD, obey him, and always be faithful. Get rid of the idols your ancestors worshiped when they lived on the other side of the Euphrates River and in Egypt. But if you don't want to worship the LORD, then choose right now! Will you worship the same idols your ancestors did? Or since you're living on land that once belonged to the Amorites, maybe you'll worship their gods. I won't. My family and I are going to worship and obey the LORD! (Jos 24:14-15).

When Bob Dylan, the folk singer popular in the 1960s and 1970s, went through his Christian phase, he wrote a 1979 song titled, "You Gotta Serve Somebody." It is a Joshua

Question kind of music. In the song, Dylan speaks to all manners of lifestyle, but one choice we all have in common is whom we will serve.

Dylan's song speaks to the essence of the "Joshua Question." Everyone everywhere chooses whom they will serve. Every parent chooses who or what they will serve, and this choice is modeled for their children. We have paraphrased the first half of Joshua 24:15 and labeled this the "Joshua Question" to remind us of the choice we must make each new day, a choice for ourselves and how we will choose to raise our kids. We hope this will be as helpful to you as it has been to us.

The Joshua Question

> Choose each day whom or what you will worship and serve. Will you worship and serve the gods of the American culture or will you worship and serve the one true God?

What Does It Mean to Say *Yes* to God?

It is time to get sold-out serious! If you say yes to God, your family life will be changed radically. Saying yes to God means getting serious about life and family priorities. It means getting serious about Proverbs 22:6. Saying yes to God means saying no to the culture's priorities.

Saying Yes to God Means Prioritizing

When we answer the "Joshua Question" with a yes to God, we are forced to prioritize our goals and expectations for our children. How many sports should our children play? What congregational programs will we participate in? How much television watching, video gaming, and instant messaging will we allow? We have created an easy-to-complete 15-item survey to help you identify the vision you have for your child. No one has to see the survey. Make a photocopy if you don't want to mark in the book.

We like to think that the statement, "I want my child to have a strong faith in Jesus Christ" gets our #1 ranking. Yet, there have been many instances where our activities do not reflect this as a high priority. Sports became too all-consuming; other activities took precedence over family time and nurturing faith. Perhaps this is true for you as well. First, do not beat yourself up. We have tried this and it has not worked as an effective strategy for passing on the faith.

Second, periodically evaluate your family priorities. We all need to do this from time to time. Use the survey as a gauge. How helpful was it in reflecting what is really important? Do you need to make changes? The gods of materialism, pleasure, power, and prestige can unexpectedly overpower our priorities and divert our faith goals for our families. If our primary goal and expectation is not centered on our faith in Jesus Christ we can unexpectedly find ourselves making other goals our gods. Third, give nurturing the faith of your family over to Christ. God is more than ready to lend a helping hand.

HomeGrown Faith Priorities Survey

Rank the following in order of importance from 1 to 15 (1 being most important to you; 2 being second most important, 3 being third most important, … 15 being least important to you).

_____ I want my child* to fit in with her/his peers.

_____ I want my child* to develop her/his talents to the fullest.

_____ I want my child* to get a good education.

_____ I want my child* to have a high self-image.

_____ I want my child* to have a strong faith in Jesus Christ.

_____ I want my child* to perform well in athletics.

_____ I want my child* to be popular.

_____ I want my child* to grow up financially secure.

_____ I want my child* to have good moral values.

_____ I want my child* to be able to get a good job.

_____ I want my child* to have a lot of fun.

_____ I want my child* to be involved in a variety of activities.

_____ I want my child* to find a good spouse.

_____ I want to fill my child's* life with the latest in technology.

_____ I want my child* to spend time with our family.

*Child includes teenagers.

Saying Yes to God Means Setting Proverbs 22:6 Priorities

Parents and grandparents have the primary responsibility for passing on the faith to children and grandchildren. Perhaps you did not know that before you began reading this book. You assumed that passing on the faith was the congregation's primary job. If you rely solely on a congregation to pass on the faith, your children may end up a statistic, one that puts them outside the four walls of a congregation when they are adults. Remember, a congregation can only supplement what is happening in your home. Connect with your kids and then connect them to Jesus.

Saying Yes to God Means Saying No to the Culture's Priorities

To choose Jesus Christ means to go counter to popular culture. This is not always an easy choice; saying yes to God means saying no to the gods of that culture. While Americans are not lifting up idols of stone or wood as was done in the Old Testament time of Joshua, we are assaulted by the gods of materialism, pleasure, power, and prestige as we mentioned before. Our culture measures our worth by how much stuff we have acquired, how much fun we experience, and how much control we wield.

One primary way the American culture assaults parents with these three false gods

Could You Do This?

Bonnie switched on the dishwasher, then turned to look at her oldest son as he came down the hall.

"Mom, there's a new show on tonight that all the kids at my school have been talking about. Would you mind if I watched it?" asked Chris.

"What's it about?" With work and taking care of the kids, Bonnie didn't have much of a chance to watch TV.

"It's a new comedy about high school," said Chris. "That's about all I know."

"Well, I guess we could give it a try."

Chris turned the TV on a few minutes before eight o'clock. His brother and sister were already getting ready for bed so it was just him and his mom. As advertised the show was about a group of kids in an affluent high school. The first few minutes were funny, but things soon changed.

"Wow," said Chris, "they really put that girl down. She didn't look that bad."

Bonnie frowned. "And do the kids at your school talk back to teachers like that?"

"Not if they want to stay in class, they don't," he said.

After watching a few more minutes, Bonnie said, "You know, Chris, I'm not comfortable at all with the way the characters are using God's name. I'm not sure that this is something you should be wasting your time on."

"I know," said Chris. "Everyone will be talking about it tomorrow and using the put-downs they are saying, but I don't think it will last very long. Let's see what else is on."

is through the goals and expectations it places on children. A dramatic shift has taken place in the expectations placed on children by our culture through the schools, the media, and out-of-school activities. The major change is that children's time is over scheduled. Structured activities, from organized sports to after-school programs, are the norm for children in the United States. Gone are the days of free time in the front yard or on the apartment stoop playing games. Less time is now spent eating, sleeping, and bathing than in past generations.

While economic pressures—such as two paycheck families, single parenting, and longer work hours—have contributed to the need for more structured activities for kids, cultural and social pressures are also responsible for the change. First, parents are busier with their own interests like self-help groups, exercise, sports, and hobbies which have given rise to the need for supervised activities for their children. Second, today's parents want their children and teenagers to excel academically, physically, socially, and emotionally so they can get ahead in life. These 21st century goals and expectations for children have unknowingly influenced American parents to worship at the altar of the gods of materialism, pleasure, power, and prestige.

What follows are six quotations that demonstrate parental goals and expectations for their children's involvement in organized activities.

"I want my daughter to be drop-dead gorgeous! That's why she is a cheerleader at six years old."

[*The god of power*]

"She loves riding and showing her horse. I just want her to be happy!"

[*The god of pleasure*]

"Sports are helping my child be a team player. That will help him get a good job.

[*The god of materialism*]

"Life is short. I want my kid to enjoy the activities I never could like camp and dance."

[*The god of pleasure*]

"I don't want my boy to be a sissy. I told him to run over anyone who gets in his way during a game."

[*The god of power*]

"I want my son to get a football scholarship to college just like I did."

[*The god of materialism*]

Answering the "Joshua Question" with a yes to God means prioritizing what we want for our children. Lofty goals and high expectations for our children can be positive. Piano lessons and soccer team practice are not inherently bad activities. Our children need us as parents to enrich their lives with healthy activities. What we must watch out for is being squeezed into the world's parenting mold. Romans 12:2 says it much better than we ever could.

Don't become so well-adjusted to your culture that you fit into it without even thinking. Instead, fix your attention on God. You'll be changed from the inside out. Readily recognize what he wants from you, and quickly respond to it. Unlike the culture around you, always dragging you down to its level of immaturity, God brings the best out of you, develops well-formed maturity in you (Ro 12:2, THE MESSAGE).

Our culture pressures us to over-involve children in the plethora of organized activities to shape their character. Overscheduled kids and families lead to unintended negative consequences, particularly a failure to nurture the Christian faith in children.

This picture of what parents want for their kids shapes the kinds of organized activities in which they participate. It also shapes the kind of faith-nurturing experiences they participate in

Parents Matter: Drug Use

A look at the research

In 2003, 14.6 million teens (58.9 percent) aged 12 to 17 reported having talked with at least one parent* during the past year about the dangers of tobacco, alcohol, or drug use.

Teens who had talked with a parent about the dangers of tobacco, alcohol, or drug use in the past year were less likely to report recent alcohol use, binge alcohol use, or illicit drug use than youths who had not.

Females (61.3 percent) were more likely to talk with a parent about the dangers of substance use than males (56.5 percent). Youths aged 12 to 13 and 14 to 15 were more likely (60.6 and 59.4 percent, respectively) to report having talked with a parent than those aged 16 or 17 (56.6 percent). The percentages of youths who reported talking with a parent about substance use varied somewhat by racial/ethnic group. White youths (61.4 percent) were more likely to report talking to a parent than black (51.2 percent), Hispanic (58.1 percent), or Asian (51.7 percent).

As a parent you make a difference. This and other studies clearly indicate that parents cannot afford to outsource their responsibility of talking with their kids to schools or congregations.

*Parents were defined as biological parents, adoptive parents, step-parents, or adult guardians whether or not they lived with the child.

"Youths' Exposure to Substance Use Prevention Messages: 2003," *The NSDUH Report.* (Office of Applied Studies, Substance Abuse and Mental Health Services Administration, July 29, 2005).

at home and within congregations. If this cultural pressure is affecting your family, sit down with your family and talk. As you create your family's *HomeGrown Faith Blueprint*, keep in mind nurturing faith and family time as priorities. You will have a chance to create your own blueprint in a few pages. A few examples follow.

Five Steps to HomeGrown Faith

You know the "Deuteronomy Promise" gives you the assurance that homegrown faith pays off. You are equipped with "The Top Ten HomeGrown Faith Practices for Parents" and understand that you can work nurturing faith into the normal routines of family life.

You are ready and willing to provide your children with a church they deserve, balancing your family life within the four ministry windows. You understand that the future does not arrive unannounced; you are the primary influencer of faith and values with your children. You have answered the "Joshua Question" with a yes to God, and you want your children to call Jesus Christ their Savior and Lord. The time has come for you to create a plan.

Pray with the end in mind

The first song my mother taught me was "Jesus Loves Me." That song speaks to the end God has in mind for our two teenage daughters. He wants them to embrace His grace.

What is God's vision for your kids? Is it that they go to every program offered in the church building? Is it perfect attendance at Sunday school? Is it that they attend every retreat and camp your congregation offers?

Or is it that they fall more and more in love with Jesus? We only need to look at the character of God to see the end for which we must pray daily. A merciful, loving God is reaching out in grace to us as broken people. Jesus spoke these words nearly 2,000 years ago and they apply to us today.

> *Everyone who has faith in the Son of Man will have eternal life. God loved the people of this world so much that he gave his only Son, so that everyone who has faith in him will have eternal life and never really die. God did not send his Son into the world to condemn its people. He sent him to save them! (Jo 3:15-17).*

Take the first step

Here are five ways you can jumpstart your homegrown faith efforts.

- If nurturing faith is not now a part of the normal routine of your family life, start with an apology. What a tremendous way to model repentance and grace with your kids.
- Start slowly. There is no need to begin all of the "Top Ten Faith Practices for Parents" in the same week. Take your time. Work what works for your family.

- If you are married, ask your spouse to pray for your kids. If your spouse is not a Christian, tell him or her you are praying for your kids.
- Grow one day at a time. Becoming anxious or feeling guilty for past parenting mistakes will not help you pass on the faith to your children. Put God first and you will be surprised how God will work in your family (Ma 6:33-34). Getting worked up over what you did not do yesterday or what you have to do tomorrow will rob you of the opportunity of touching the lives of your children today.
- Rely on the Holy Spirit who lives within you for strength and guidance. (See John 14:16-17; Romans 5:5; 1 Corinthians 6:19.)

Try an experiment

Our challenge to you: Try a homegrown faith experiment. Here is our "HomeGrown Faith Blueprint" that can help you plan a homegrown faith strategy for your family. Because each family is unique, no single plan will work. Our family has found that, when we create our own plan, we are more likely to follow through with it. Why not give the blueprint a try with your family?

The "HomeGrown Faith Blueprint" shown in Figure One takes four of the "Top Ten Home-Grown Faith Practices for Parents" and places them in relationship to mealtimes. Each of the four practices—Caring Conversations, Family Devotions, Family Prayer, and Family Acts of Service—can be done at shared family mealtimes. Revelation 3:20 gives us a picture of Jesus knocking at the door of the church. *Listen! I am standing and knocking at your door. If you hear my voice and open the door, I will come in and we will eat together.* Jesus is standing at the door of your *little church* called home, the domestic church. He wants you to invite Him in to your mealtime.

The completed blueprint, shown in Figure Two, gives you an idea of what your mealtimes could look like with Jesus participating. This is also an example of how you can

Could You Do This?

Sam called out to his wife Liz, who was in the kitchen popping corn. "Honey, come on! The game is about to start!"

"Yeah, Mom, hurry up!" Louie dropped down on the sofa with a bounce. "You'll miss the tip-off."

The Collins family enjoyed watching college sports together, and this was the game that would decide if their team would make it to the playoffs.

"Okay, okay!" Liz brought the popcorn in from the kitchen. "Tell them they can start now."

"Mom," said Dan, rolling his eyes.

With their team in the lead by four points, a commercial interrupted the game. It featured a group of beautiful girls and good-looking guys at a party together. The center of their attention was a new brand of beer. According to the commercial, if you drank this particular beer, you would be as good-looking and popular as the people in the commercial.

"I wish they wouldn't do that," said Sam to his wife.

"What's that?" she asked.

"Make it look like drinking makes you popular. I think that gives the wrong message to kids who watch sports on TV."

"I don't see how you can be a good athlete and drink," said Dan. He had just started playing basketball on his middle-school team and was learning how demanding sports could be.

"You can't," said his mom, "but they sure use it to sell more beer."

"Let's just watch the game, then turn it off during commercials," Carla suggested.

"Good idea, kiddo," said Sam.

Figure One

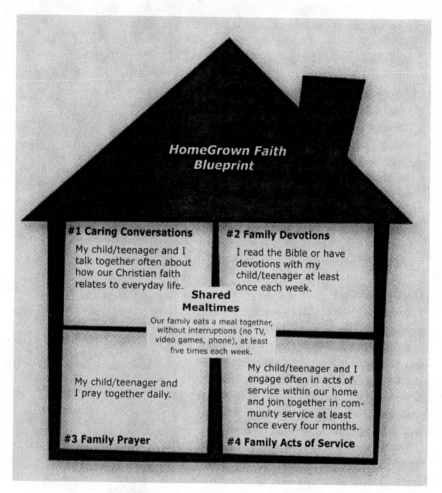

HomeGrown Faith Blueprint

#1 Caring Conversations

My child/teenager and I talk together often about how our Christian faith relates to everyday life.

#2 Family Devotions

I read the Bible or have devotions with my child/teenager at least once each week.

Shared Mealtimes

Our family eats a meal together, without interruptions (no TV, video games, phone), at least five times each week.

My child/teenager and I pray together daily.

My child/teenager and I engage often in acts of service within our home and join together in community service at least once every four months.

#3 Family Prayer

#4 Family Acts of Service

work nurturing faith into a normal routine of family life. If you are not sharing meals as a family, we implore you to find ways to work this into your family routine. As difficult as they may be, this family ritual will build up and strengthen your family in ways that you cannot imagine. By inviting Jesus to your mealtimes, you have the added benefit of energizing your family's faith.

Once family mealtimes with Jesus have become a routine in your family, you can use the blueprint to add faith formation into other family routines. Figure Three gives you an example of what this might look like.

Now it is time to develop your own family's blueprint. Figure Four shows a blank blueprint. Reconstruct this on a piece of paper and invite your family to sit down with you and draft your own plan.

Figure Two

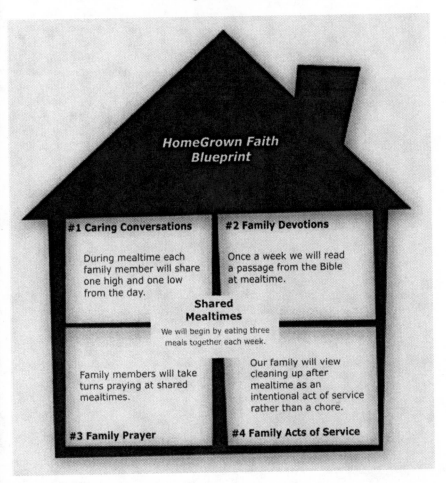

Identify your potential roadblocks

Your family will encounter obstacles as you try to implement your "HomeGrown Faith Blueprint." Look at the following roadblocks, identify those that could affect your family, and decide ahead of time what you and your family can do to overcome them. You may have additional roadblocks to add to this list.

- Change moves us out of our comfort zone. It will be easy to drift into old routines.
- The kids do not like change.
- My spouse is not a Christian.
- Our family watches too much television.

Figure Three

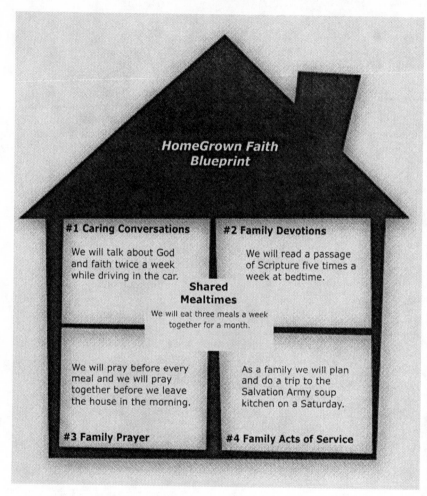

- Video games rule in our house.
- I am afraid I will not know what to do.
- I feel guilty for not doing homegrown faith in the past.

Grow for it!

Kids need to be raised physically, spiritually, emotionally, and mentally. Raising kids requires a hands-on approach that is sometimes tough. Remember, homegrown faith is about eternity. Do not give up. It is about Jesus. If what you do does not work, try something else. Keep trying caring conversations, devotions, prayer, and family acts of service until they are no longer awkward but are part of the normal routine of your family life.

Figure Four

HomeGrown Faith
Blueprint

A Bible Passage to Remember

Obey God's message! Don't fool yourselves by just listening to it. If you hear the message and don't obey it, you are like people who stare at themselves in a mirror and forget what they look like as soon as they leave (Ja 1:22-24).

A Thought to Consider

The main thing is to keep the main thing the main thing—and the main thing is Jesus.

A Question to Ask Yourself

Are you willing to do whatever it takes to pass on the Christian faith to your children?

Parents Matter: Driving

A look at the research

Data from the North Carolina Driver History File matched the driving records of 18 to 21-year-olds with that of their parents. The result was a strong correlation between the accident rates of moms and dads and their offspring.

Susan A. Ferguson, Allan F. Williams, Janella F. Chapline, Donald W. Reinfurt, and Doreen M. De Leonardis, "Relationship of parent driving records to the driving records of their children," *Accident Analysis & Prevention*, (33.2, March 1, 2001), 229-234.

Dialogue Questions for Group Study

Jumpstart a healthy homegrown faith dialogue in your Sunday school class or small group with the following questions. You can also use "A Bible Passage to Remember," "A Thought to Consider," and "A Question to Ask Yourself" at the end of each chapter to spark a lively discussion.

1. How will you answer the Joshua Question for your family?
2. What did the *HomeGrown Faith Priorities Survey* reveal to you?
3. How is family time a priority in your family? How can you connect with your kids in a way that makes Proverbs 22:6 happen?
4. What were potential obstacles that you identified that could block the implementation of your *HomeGrown Faith Blueprint?*
5. How could your family use the *HomeGrown Faith Blueprint* beyond nurturing faith at mealtime?

Chapter Six

Grandparents* Passing on the Faith

Parents: Ask your kids' grandparents to read this chapter!

Someday your children will ask, "Why are these rocks here?" Then you can tell them how the water stopped flowing when the chest was being carried across the river. These rocks will always remind our people of what happened here today (Jos 4:6).

The Goodman Family

Anna sat down to read her Bible while the boys were taking their naps. Anna really enjoyed this quiet time. As much as she enjoyed caring for her grandsons during the day, it could get quite hectic.

Turning to the passage for the day, she began to read:

And Eliud begat Eleazar; and Eleazar begat Matthan; and Matthan begat Jacob; and Jacob begat Joseph the husband of Mary, of whom was born Jesus, who is called Christ (Ma 1:15-16, KJV).

"Well, my word." She read the verses again.

"I never thought about it before, but Jesus had a grandpa. Jacob was Joseph's father so that made him Jesus' grandpa! Grandpa Jake!" Anna imagined little Jesus sitting on Grandpa Jacob's lap listening to stories about His family. The image brought a smile to her face. She could see Him as a little boy, much like her grandson Joey. "Jacob probably even talked with Jesus about spiritual things and told him about God just like I talk to the boys."

Just thinking about it made Anna want to talk with her grandsons even more about spiritual things. Anna thought of the fun she had with her own grandsons and her opportunity to teach them about the faith. Her son and daughter-in-law encouraged her to do this, saying it was one more way the boys could learn about Jesus. Anna smiled; she wasn't just the boys' babysitter; she made a real difference in their lives!

"I wish other grandparents realized how important they are in the lives of their grandkids," Anna thought. Many of her friends didn't even see their grandchildren for months at a time, and those who did see them probably didn't talk much about their faith. "What a wasted opportunity."

*If you are a grandparent raising your grandchildren, don't stop with this chapter, read the rest of the book.

Anna heard a noise down the hall and knew she would soon hear the sound of little footsteps coming her direction. Nap time, and her quiet time, were over. This afternoon she and the boys were making cookies, so she knew that the rest of the afternoon would be busy.

"Did you miss us, Grandma?" Joey rubbed his eyes. He worried about Anna being lonely when they weren't around.

"I missed you bunches," she said and gave him a big hug.

"Were you reading?" Matt asked.

"Yes, I was reading a story about Jesus when He was a little boy," she said, scooping Joey up into her lap.

"Jesus was a little boy once?" Joey asked skeptically.

Matt rolled his eyes. "Of course, he was," he said. "Remember, He was born on Christmas, so He had to be little sometime."

"Oh, right." Joey processed this information.

"And I learned something," said Anna.

Could You Do This?

When the boys had finished helping their Grandma Anna load groceries into the car, they climbed in and put on their seatbelts.

"I can't wait to get to your house, Grandma," said Matt. "We haven't made cookies in a long time."

"Well, your dad will really appreciate you making them for his birthday," said Anna.

As they pulled onto the busy street, Anna noticed the flashing of emergency vehicle lights, lots of them. "Oh, my. It looks like there is a big traffic accident up ahead."

She slowed down and drove in the direction that the sheriff was pointing. She could see that at least three people had been injured badly enough to be waiting for ambulances to transport them to the hospital. "Boys, I think those people need us to pray for them," she said. "Would one of you like to pray?"

"I will, Grandma," said Joey. He folded his hands and scrunched his eyes closed. "Dear Lord. Please take care of those people that were in that accident back there. Help them to get better. Amen." He looked up at Anna. "How was that?"

"That was great, Joey," said Anna. "I'm sure the Lord was listening."

"What?" Matt asked.

"I learned that Jesus had grandparents. He had a grandpa named Jacob."

"Do you think they made cookies and went to the park?" Joey asked, remembering they were making cookies later.

"I bet they did lots of things together." She kissed Joey on the top of the head and set him down. "Let's get you guys a drink and get out the stuff to make cookies."

"Great," said Matt. "So what was Jesus' grandpa's name again?"

"Jacob," said Anna. "His name was Grandpa Jake."

Grandparenting is Vital

Grandparents, you have a gift to give to your grandchildren. It's not a new video game or doll, but an eternal gift of faith. You have the privilege of energizing your grandchildren's faith. The role of grandparents in leaving a legacy of faith is recorded in Scripture, in the Old Testament Book of Deuteronomy.

*You must be very careful not to forget the things you have seen God do for you. Keep reminding yourselves, and tell your children and **grandchildren** as well (De 4:9).*

The first half of this verse explains how adults, parents, and grandparents can best live their lives—remembering all that God has done. The second half of the verse pleads with grandparents to share their God story with their grandchildren. Talk about those times God healed you, when He rescued you from a tough situation, or when He walked with you through a desperate and frightful time. Talk about all the ways God has worked in your life.

It is not enough for your children alone to tell their stories to your grandchildren. Faith is caught much more than it is taught. God's plan for passing on the faith is what we call the "Deuteronomy Promise."

God's wonderful plan for living by faith is best passed on to children, including teenagers, through the home within the normal routines of family life so that kids and their parents (and extended family) can together experience the joy of living in grace as they follow Christ and so that these kids as adults will choose to be Christ-followers. (See Deuteronomy 6:4-7, 20-25; 11:1-28; 32:46-47.)

You can assist your grandchildren's parents as they pass on the faith by telling stories of God, Christ, and the Bible as part of the normal routines of grandparenting. In today's world, your grandchildren need all the faith stories they can get from you. In his second letter to his disciple Timothy, the apostle Paul mentions the influence Timothy's grandmother had on her daughter Eunice and her grandson Timothy.

I also remember the genuine faith of your mother Eunice. Your grandmother Lois had the same sort of faith, and I am sure that you have it as well (2 Ti 1:5).

Sounds like Grandma Lois spent some time in the rocking chair talking with her grandkids about the faith!

Grandparents have always played an important role in raising healthy grandkids, but now they are more important than ever. In many families, parents are stretched to the breaking point; there is just not enough time to do it all. Kids are also being bombarded by a culture that tells them things of the world are more important than things of the faith. So what is a grandparent to do? Respond to the "Ezekiel Call." That is our name for God's call to grandparents who come alongside their grandkids and build them up in Christ in the midst of a culture attempting to tear them apart. In the Old Testament time of the prophet Ezekiel, God looked for someone to protect and defend the people who were being treated unjustly.

God spoke to the people through Ezekiel: "The people themselves cheat and rob; they abuse the poor and take advantage of foreigners. I looked for someone to defend the city and to protect it from my anger, as well as to stop me from destroying it. But I found no one" (Ez 22:29-30).

What is God's Ezekiel Call asking you to do as you pass on the Christian faith to your grandchildren and maybe even great-grandchildren?

Roadblocks You May Face

For some grandparents, getting involved in the lives of their grandkids is not always smooth sailing; there may be problems from distance to divorce. Whatever roadblocks you face, a good rule to follow is no matter what, think of your grandchildren and how you can best be involved in their lives.

Differing Beliefs

"But," you may say, "my grandchildren are being raised in a home where one of their parents is not a Christian. How can I possibly pass on faith to them?" Live out Christ every day in front of your children and your grandchildren. Realize that you are a reflection of Christ each time they see or talk to you. You do not have to preach to them to share your faith. They will see your faith in the loving way you treat them and how you handle difficult situations or change. Your grandchildren will also hear it in the stories you tell about your childhood and feel it through your compassion to others. They will see Christ through you in your unconditional love and forgiveness.

A Lot of Grandparents

A generation ago, grandparents had many grandkids; today, kids have a lot of grandparents. A child can easily have four parents and up to eight grandparents with divorce, step-parenting, and step-grandparenting. Take an active role in your grandchildren's lives no matter how many other grandparents they may have. You have a tremendous responsibility and an awesome privilege to teach your grandchild the ways of faith. The apostle Peter calls Christians "living stones." *And now you are living stones that are being used to build a spiritual house (1 Pe 2:5a).* As a living stone, you can lay a spiritual foundation for your grandchildren.

Parenting Instead of Grandparenting

Here is a tough one. Many times it is difficult for a grandparent not to parent. You may not agree with your adult child's parenting style, but the important thing is to support them. Do not discuss the situation with your grandkids or talk negatively about their parents. If you must discuss a parenting issue with your children, do it out of hearing range of your grandkids. Give these issues to God (Ph 4:6-7; 1 Pe 5:7) and stick with grandparenting!

Distance

In our mobile society, it is not unusual for grandparents to live a city or a nation away from their grandchildren. Does this present a challenge when it comes to being an influence in the lives of your grandchildren? Of course. Is it worth the extra effort to try? Most definitely. With a little creativity, you can be just as involved with grandchildren who live far away as you are with ones nearby. Contact them through phone calls, instant messaging, e-mails, video, and DVD recordings. Be creative, but stay in contact with them.

Not Allowed Contact

For whatever reason, perhaps you are not allowed to see your grandchildren. Prayer is the most powerful strategy you have as a grandparent, whether or not you see them in person. Ask your friends and your congregation to do the same.

Build Lasting Memories

With more of life behind than there is ahead, it is often easier for grandparents to look to the past than to the future. Take your past and touch the future by creating lasting memories that can shape the character and faith of your grandchildren.

Stories

A grandparent is like a living history book; you carry with you the stories from the past. Your grandchildren will never tire of hearing stories about your childhood and about other family members they will never know. Share your favorite Bible stories, verses, or events in your life that have strengthened your faith in God. If your grandchildren are not near you, these stories can be taped or written and mailed.

Milestones

Celebrate and affirm your grandchildren's faith at every major step of their lives. At each of these milestones, you can praise and thank God for working in their lives. Any of the following events in your grandchildren's lives can be a cause for celebration. Make a memory of each of these events that includes a God memory, and give it to your children as a keepsake.

- Birth and each birthday
- Starting kindergarten, elementary, middle and high school
- Baptism/Baby dedication
- First Bible
- Confirmation
- First Communion
- Driver's license

- Dating
- Graduations
- Wedding

Special Verse

Choose a Bible verse to remember each of your grandchildren. This could be a verse that has encouraged you. Write the child's name and his verse on a card and keep it inside your Bible so you see it every time you pray or read your Bible. You can also write it on the inside cover or blank pages of your Bible to have them handy. Use this as a reminder to pray for your grandchild. Share the verse with him and explain why you chose that particular verse.

Scrapbooking

Popular in previous generations as a way to preserve memories and pass on faith and values, a scrapbook makes a wonderful keepsake for your grandkids. Here are a few ideas to include in a grandchild's scrapbook:

- Pictures of you along with stories of your faith journey.
- Pictures of you at faith milestones, such as pictures of your baptism.
- Pictures of relatives whom they know, along with stories of their faith journey.
- Pictures of relatives who have died. If they were Christians, include their faith stories.
- Pictures of your grandkids at milestones in their lives, along with your memories of the events.
- Favorite Bible verses. Include a narrative about why this verse means so much to you.
- A list of favorite Bible stories. Include the passages and why you like them.
- Throughout the scrapbook, include a narrative of your personal faith journey. Include times when you felt close to God and those times when you didn't. Describe any major decisions or disappointments in your life and how God helped you with them. These could include choice of friends, career, and spouse. You don't need to go into great detail about the event. Place your emphasis on God's role in seeing you through.
- You can also include faith stories of other family members who were influential on your family. Maybe you had an aunt who was a missionary or a hard-working, hard-praying great-grandpa who kept the family together in hard times.
- Pictures can also be used to document your relationship with your grandchild. Place them in chronological order so that she can see herself growing and how you have been there with her on the journey. You can also make a scrapbook with ticket stubs, play programs, maps, and other souvenirs from your times together.

Now you have turned a simple scrapbook into a tool for talking about your faith. Share the scrapbook often with your grandchild as you document his faith journey. This scrapbook can become a keepsake gift for him on a special birthday.

Cousins' Party

Have more than one grandchild? Then you have an amazing opportunity to create a memory for all of them by having a cousins' party. Let it be a giant slumber party with people who love them. You can make popcorn, show home movies, tell stories, play games, and make or buy all their favorite foods. Tell stories about family members they may not know or remember. Pray together as a group or if there are a lot of cousins, break into smaller groups with older and younger cousins mixed. The younger ones will have wonderful spiritual role models and the older ones will recognize the awesome responsibility they have to be those role models. Take pictures or make a video to preserve the event. They'll talk about this visit for years.

Trips

A trip to the hardware store may just be routine to you, but taking a grandchild with you opens up a whole new world. Not only will you see things in a new way, but she will be thrilled to be included. Take her places you normally go like the library, the lake, the beauty shop, or the grocery store. Use this time together to learn more about her world. Ask questions and be willing to answer them. These are times to savor with your grandchild, not just rush about to do errands. Make the focus a time to build your relationship.

Leave a Legacy of Faith

Heirloom Faith

Listening to the stories of grandparents helps grandchildren feel connected to something beyond themselves. Talk about your memories of Bible stories your parents told you or interesting

Could You Do This?

Bonnie sighed as she looked at the calendar. "I can't believe it."

"What's wrong?" Her husband Frank got up and walked over to where she was standing in the kitchen.

"I just realized that we haven't eaten together as a family in over three weeks!" said Bonnie.

"No way," said Frank. "It can't be that long."

"Look." She pointed to the calendar. Each day for the last three weeks was packed full with activities for each of them. "We haven't been home together since the barbeque we had at the beginning of the month."

"The kids always seem to have so much to do, and I always have to work late these days. It does seem like we can never get together for dinner," said Frank.

"I know," said Bonnie, "but with the kids getting older, we have less time together as a family. I think it's important for the kids that we get together more."

"Okay, I agree," said Frank, "but just how do we work this when we're so busy?"

Bonnie looked at the calendar again, tapping her lips with a pencil. "Okay. We really can't have dinner together for the next few weeks, but we could get up at the same time and have breakfast together. We could at least start the day with each other, you know, sit down, say grace together, the whole thing."

Frank laughed. "This could be a problem for Chris. You know he likes to sleep in during the summer."

Bonnie grinned. "So he can go back to sleep after breakfast."

"You really think this is that important?" Frank asked.

"Yeah, I do," she said. "I feel like we are losing touch with our family. If we can eat five or six meals together each week, maybe we can feel more like a family and less like roommates."

"Okay," said Frank. "Let's tell the kids that we have a date for breakfast tomorrow morning."

ways you prayed when you were young. Say the prayers you learned as a child and teach them to your grandchildren. Talk about how they will someday share these prayers with their children and grandchildren.

Baby Love

Holding your grandbaby ranks high on a grandparent's list of favorite things to do. Use this time to share your faith with this special little one. Pick up your grandchild and walk around your home (or his home) and point to things that make you or your grandchild happy. Say, "This makes me happy, and God wants us to be happy." Simply saying, "I love you, and God loves you," when you pick up your grandchild will share God's love with the child in a special way.

Sacred Space

Create a special spot in your home that is just for her, a place she knows will be waiting every time she visits. It could be a corner in the den that has a shelf with her things or a comfy bean bag chair for her to sit on as you talk, read Bible stories, pray together, or just cuddle. She will know that she has a special place in your home as well as your heart.

Copycats

Let your grandkids be copycats and give them something to copy. Let them see you reading the Bible, praying, participating in a congregation, listening to or singing worship songs, forgiving others, or helping others. Let them see the faith in your life; don't just tell them about it. Look for ways to nurture their faith. Realize that you are a symbol of their hope in Jesus Christ through your own attitudes and actions. By doing these things you leave an inheritance to your grandchildren—a spiritual inheritance.

Gifts

You like to buy gifts for your grandchildren. Why not make it an opportunity to provide your grandchildren with resources to develop their faith? Consider age-appropriate Bibles, books, music, and videos. Be the resource of inspiration for your grandchildren.

Mentor

Be a mentor for your grandchildren. Be there to ask questions and then talk with them about their answers. Be available to listen or to help them look for information they may need to make good decisions.

Verse Ritual

Create a tradition by talking about a Bible verse. Use a devotional, and share verses you have found important. Ask him what he thinks the verse means, and share what it means to you. Have fun by challenging older grandchildren to memorize the verse with you.

Bubble Prayers

Another fun way to share your faith with a small child is with a bottle of bubble solution. As you blow bubbles together, tell your grandchild the bubbles are like prayers floating up to heaven. Blow bubbles together and say simple prayers like, "God bless Mommy and Daddy" or "Thank you for my puppy."

Coloring

Kids love to draw and color, and they really enjoy doing it with someone they love. You can use this love of art to encourage a young child's faith. Draw pictures of Bible stories, characters, or places such as the garden of Eden, Noah's ark, heaven, David and Goliath. The list is endless. It might also be interesting to see what your grandchild's perception of God and Jesus are by asking him to draw a picture of what he thinks they look like. Compare your pictures and talk about each other's artwork. Focus on content rather than on artistic ability.

Encourage Meaningful Talk

Once upon a time grandparents lived with or near their grandchildren. It was not unusual to see Grandma working around the house or Grandpa fishing with the kids. What a time that must have been, to be able to talk with your grandchildren whenever you wanted to. Times change and now thousands of miles may separate grandparents from their grandchildren. Here are some hints to encourage vital communication with your grandchildren.

- Keep things positive.
- Talk on their level about things that interest them.
- Show your interest in their lives.
- Have fun with current methods of communication: e-mail, voice mail, text messages, etc.
- Send an old-fashioned letter—everyone likes to get mail.
- Keep up on current events and trends to discuss.
- Become familiar with your grandchild's favorite TV shows, books, and music.

- The most important tip to encourage meaningful talk with your grandchild—listen! You are a source of unconditional love whom she can talk to about anything.

A Bible Passage to Remember

You must be very careful not to forget the things you have seen God do for you. Keep reminding yourselves, and tell your children and grandchildren as well (De 4:9).

A Thought to Consider

Grandparents can be more influential than coaches, teachers, mentors, counselors, pastors, or Sunday school teachers in energizing the faith and values of their grandchildren.

A Question to Ask Yourself

What are your responsibilities in passing on the Christian faith to your grandchildren?

Dialogue Questions for Group Study

Jumpstart a healthy homegrown faith dialogue in your Sunday school class or small group with the following questions. You can also use "A Bible Passage to Remember," "A Thought to Consider," and "A Question to Ask Yourself" at the end of each chapter to spark a lively discussion.

1. What role would you like to play in nurturing faith in your grandchildren?
2. What methods have you used to communicate with your grandchildren? What new ones would you be willing to learn?
3. If you could impart any faith lesson to your grandchild, what would it be?
4. What obstacles might you face in nurturing faith in your grandchildren?
5. What do you plan to do differently this week to communicate with your grandchild?

Fifty Nifty HomeGrown Faith Activities You Can Do with Your Kids and Grandkids

Chapter Seven

Imaginative Prayer Ideas That Get Kids' Attention!

God gave his Law to Jacob's descendants, the people of Israel. And he told our ancestors to teach their children, so that each new generation would know his Law and tell it to the next. Then they would trust God and obey his teachings, without forgetting anything God had done (Ps 78:5-7).

I'm Sorry—Thank You—Help Me—Please

"...and help Aunt Carol to feel better. Amen." Jesse finished his prayer.

"You forgot to say 'please.'" His dad smiled.

"Dad, I'm just praying."

"Just praying? I think that talking to the God of the universe deserves a little more than 'just praying,' don't you?"

"I never thought of it that way." Jesse sat back from the table.

"You know, I never did either," his mom offered, "but I did teach you to have manners when you talk to other people. I think God definitely deserves our politeness."

"How can you be polite to God?" Jesse wondered out loud. The thought of having to remember to say all the right words made him a bit uncomfortable.

"Just use the words we taught you to use when you talk with other people."

Jesse thought for a minute, then said, "You taught me to say 'please' and 'thank you.'"

"That's right," his mom answered, "and I bet God would like to hear those words too."

"OK," Jesse said. "That's two. I wonder what else God would want to hear?"

"I know I always feel better when I hear the words, 'I'm sorry' if someone has done or said something that hurts my feelings."

"I never thought about God having feelings before," Jesse said. "I probably should be saying 'I'm sorry' a lot more."

Jesse's dad laughed. "I don't think you're quite that bad. But I know God would appreciate the thought."

"I have another one." His mom stood up from the table to clear the dishes. "How about 'help me'? There are times during the day when I could use a little help."

"So 'please,' 'thank you,' 'help me,' and 'I'm sorry,'" Jesse repeated. "I hope God likes good manners."

Could You Do This?

"What are you doing, Mom?" asked Jenna as she walked into the family room. Her mother Bonnie was sitting on the couch with a book in her lap.

"Oh, I'm just updating your scrapbook." Bonnie smoothed a picture down on one of the pages.

Jenna looked at the picture her mother was adding to the book. "Hey, that's me at the Vacation Bible School program."

"You did a really good job in the skit that your group performed."

"I liked acting out Bible stories," said Jenna, "but why are you putting it in my scrapbook. I thought only special things went in there." Jenna knew her mom kept a scrapbook for all of her kids, but she thought that only really important stuff went in them, like awards and school pictures.

"This *is* special. I don't just put things about your mental and physical accomplishments. I like to put things in about your spiritual growth, too."

"Like what?"

"Well ..." Bonnie turned the pages of the book. "I have the certificate from your baptism and the ribbon you got for being an outstanding singer in the children's choir...."

"Mom," said Jenna, rolling her eyes. "We all got ribbons just for being in the choir."

"I know, I know, but I wanted to put that in because you enjoyed it so much. I also have a picture from the day you got your Bible from the church and from Christmas programs you have been in."

"What are those?" Jenna pointed at one of the pages.

"Those are verses that you have learned in Sunday school, or ones that I picked out for you. I thought it would be nice to look back on them and see some verses that were special to you when you were growing up."

Jenna looked closer. "Wow," she said, "I can remember most of them!"

"Good for you, Jenna," said her mom.

Jenna hugged Bonnie. "Thanks, Mom."

"For what, sweetie?" said Bonnie.

"For keeping track of all the important things in my life," she said.

"No problem," said Bonnie, as she hugged Jenna back.

Fifty Nifty Idea #1

I'm sorry! Thank you! Help me! Please! Simple but important words we use to convey respect. These same words can be used when we talk to God, giving direction to your family's prayer time.

Write the following incomplete phrases on a card or sheet of paper:

- I'm sorry ...
- Thank you ...
- Help me ...
- Please ...

Have it handy at your next family prayer time—at a mealtime or before bed. Use these phrases to guide your prayers. Ask each family member to pick at least one prayer starter.

I'm sorry ... Start your prayer with confession. Give to God any sins you have committed, and ask for forgiveness.

Thank you ... Offer a prayer of gratitude for your family, your home, a new job, or someone recovering from an illness.

Help me ... Here's the time when you make your requests of God. He is waiting to help you with your problems.

Please ... What are your concerns or requests for others? Perhaps they sound like these: "Lord, please help my sister pass her test," or "please God, help my grandma with her sadness from losing Grandpa."

Say "Amen" together, and put the prayer card where it will be easy to find to guide you through your next prayer time together.

Prayer Field Trip

"Mom, what's this piece of paper on the bathroom counter for? It says 'Health of the Family,'" Dana asked.

"Oh that's something for our prayer field trip around the house that we will be doing later," her mom answered.

"Oh. What? Wait a minute, what are you talking about? We're going to pray in the bathroom? That's weird, Mom," Dana turned away from the counter toward her mother's voice.

"I just thought it would be fun to do something different for our family prayer time, so we're going from room to room praying about the topic we find there."

"OK, that could work," said Dana. "But if any of my friends ask what we did tonight, I don't know if I'll tell them that we were praying in the bathroom!"

Fifty Nifty Idea #2

Is your family prayer time becoming too predictable? Do you always pray in the same location? If your answers are "yes," then it is time to jumpstart your prayer time with a prayer field trip around your home. It doesn't take much preparation for you to put some new life into this vital time together.

Before beginning your prayer time, designate each room in your home to a specific prayer concern. Write each of these concerns on a sheet of paper and place it in that room. For example, write "Health of our family" and place it on the bathroom counter; "Friends and family" and place it on a couch or chair in the living room; "Food and stuff" and place this on the kitchen counter; and "Forgiveness, peace, and trust" and place it on a bed in a bedroom.

Say to your family, "We are going on a prayer field trip to different rooms in our home. In each room, we will find a sheet of paper that will tell us what we are to pray for there.

Proceed to pray your way through each of the rooms. Hold hands as you pray together. You can have a different person pray in each room or each person pray in every room.

Prayer Toss-Up

"Oh, great," thought Kyle. "Here we go again. I wonder where my dad gets this stuff."

Kyle's dad had just finished explaining a new way of praying that he wanted the family to try.

"And then we will toss our prayers to heaven and say, 'Lord, hear our prayers!'" Kyle's father said excitedly.

"Oh, well, might as well do it and get it over with." Kyle sat down at the kitchen table.

Soon Kyle was caught up in the prayers of his family members. Then it was his turn to pray. Usually Kyle was uncomfortable about praying out loud, but this time he didn't mind.

After everyone had "tossed" their prayers to God, Kyle turned to his father and said, "Hey, that was pretty cool!"

Fifty Nifty Idea #3

Prayer time can be an adventure for your family. Just remember you are talking to our awesome God. Since He gave us our creativity; use it to energize your prayer life.

Of course we don't want our way of praying to be flippant or disrespectful, but that doesn't mean we shouldn't enjoy our family prayer time. "Prayer Toss-Up" is just one more way to encourage your family members to have an active prayer life.

Ask your family members to sit in a circle either on the floor, at a table, or in a circle of chairs.

Say, "Each time we pray, we send those prayers up to heaven. This prayer activity called 'Prayer Toss-Up' will let us physically do that." Consider with your family members the prayers they would like to toss up to God. These could include requests and praises.

Often we fold our hands to pray, but for this activity, ask each family member to speak their prayers into their cupped hands. If the prayer is very personal, it can be said silently.

When the last family member has finished praying, ask them all on the count of three to throw their prayers to heaven, saying, "Lord, hear our prayers."

Chocolate-Dipped Prayers

"Wow, Mom, chocolate chips! Are we making cookies?" Laura looked at the ingredients on the kitchen counter.

"No, not cookies," her mom answered. "We're going to make something for our prayer time tonight."

"I think I'm going to like this," said Laura. "So, what are we going to do with the chocolate?"

"We're going to melt it and dip pretzels into it." Her mom put some chocolate chips in a saucepan.

"Sounds great, but I'm not getting the connection to prayer here," said Laura.

"Well, Laura, did you know that pretzels are all about prayer?" her mom asked.

"Nope," said Laura, "never heard that before."

"It's true." She turned on the burner. "Over a thousand years ago a monk was making bread to be used during Lent. In those days, it was common for Christians to pray by crossing their hands over their chests and touching their shoulders. The monk formed the dough into what we now know as a pretzel by rolling the dough into a long rope and crossing the ends over so that they touched the opposite 'shoulder' of the pretzels. These were called *pretiola* and were given to children as rewards for learning their prayers."

"I didn't know that. So when did he start dipping them in chocolate?"

"He didn't, that part was my idea." Her mom smiled.

Fifty Nifty Idea #4

Whether you teach the story of how the pretzel began or you use another story, the time spent with your family making this treat will interest everyone in your family. Gather the family together. Before you begin, pray together thanking God for your great family and for the opportunity you have to pray together with them and for them. Then get busy making a batch of chocolate-covered prayers.

For this prayer activity, you will need to gather the following:

- Two 12 oz. bags of dark, semi-sweet, or milk chocolate chips
- One bag of small pretzels
- One tablespoon margarine or butter
- A microwave-safe bowl
- Tongs (optional)
- Spoon
- Waxed paper

Put the margarine and the chocolate chips into a bowl and microwave them for one minute. Stir the mixture. If there are any unmelted chocolate chips, microwave the mixture for 15 seconds and stir. Continue this process until all chocolate chips have melted.

Dip the pretzels, one at a time, into the chocolate using a spoon or tongs. Place the pretzels on the waxed paper. Continue until all the pretzels are covered.

Note: If the chocolate in the bowl begins to harden, microwave it for 15 seconds and stir.

Before eating the pretzels, take time to pray together as a family the way the early Christians did by crossing your arms over your chest and touching your shoulders. After praying, enjoy eating this meaningful snack.

Variation: This recipe can also be made on top of the stove by using a double boiler. Pour the chocolate chips into a smaller pan and place in a larger pan filled with water. As the water heats, the chocolate will melt. Stir frequently.

Caution: All cooking with children should be done under adult supervision.

Life-Sized Friendship Prayers

"OK, Sam, it's your turn to pray tonight," Cal said to his son Sam. Usually Dad did the praying before they went to bed, but recently he had started encouraging Sam to pray, too.

Sam folded his hands and bowed his head. After a few quiet moments, he opened his eyes, "I don't know what to pray for, Dad. When you pray it seems so easy, but when I close my eyes and try to pray I just can't think of anything."

"It is important that you learn how to pray, Sam. What we need is a way to help you think of the things that you want to pray for."

"Like a picture in my brain, right?" Sam asked hopefully.

"That's a good way to put it," his dad answered. "Go get me the newspaper and I'll show you what we're going to do."

Fifty Nifty Idea #5

Praying can be hard for kids sometimes because they can't "see" the things they are praying for. This activity turns abstract prayers into concrete images children can visualize while they are praying. Plus, making the prayer reminder provides a fun way to be creative.

For this activity, you will need the following materials:

- Large sheet of paper or newspaper taped together
- Pencil
- Washable marker
- Scissors
- Glue or glue stick
- Slips of paper or sticky-backed notes
- Tape
- Copies of pictures of friends, family members and pets

Tape together pieces of paper to make a sheet as large as your child; ask your child to lie down on the paper while you draw her outline with a waterproof marker. Cut around the outline or have her do the cutting if she is able.

Tape the body outline to an open area of wall in her bedroom or in another available space. To this outline you will be taping or gluing pictures or notes with names of prayer requests. Help your child cut out photographs, draw pictures, or write names of people, pets, or items for which she would like to pray. Glue or tape these to the outline.

Pray near the outline. Ask her to name the things or people she wants to pray for. Remove items as requests are answered and add new things as desired.

Remembering the Cross Prayers

Derek looked at the picture of Jesus on the cross that was in his new Bible. "That must have really hurt," he said to himself.

Overhearing him, his aunt asked, "What are you looking at?"

"This picture of Jesus on the cross," said Derek. "I just realized how much that must have hurt."

"Yeah, Jesus really must love us a lot to go through that much pain."

"But He didn't have to," said Derek. "He was God's Son!"

"True. But I think Jesus did it so we would know just what He would go through to show us how much He loved us," Derek's aunt said.

"I don't feel like I show Jesus how much I love him very often." Derek looked dejected.

"Sure you do," said his aunt. "Every time you pray or praise God, you show how much you care. And when you share or care about others."

"I guess."

"I know a way you can pray that will help you feel like you are closer to God," she said. "It's called a 'Cross Prayer.' Let me show you how to do it."

Fifty Nifty Idea #6

Remembering the crucifixion is not fun. Christ died a gruesome, painful death. Early Christians prayed with their arms outstretched, like they were hanging on the cross, as a way to remember how Christ suffered to pay for their sins. This rather uncomfortable way of praying can be used to help your family physically remember the price Christ paid.

Demonstrate for your family how they will be praying during this time. Relax your body before you begin. Gently shake your arms and hands, and gently rotate your neck. Take slow, deep breaths as you do this.

Close your eyes as you stretch your arms out to your sides as if you were hanging on a cross. Look up and then slowly close your eyes. Ask your family to join you in this position. Try to remain this way throughout the entire prayer.

Your prayers may be spoken out loud or silently. Begin your prayer time by confessing your sins. Realize your powerlessness over these sins without God's help.

As you are praying, be aware of how your body feels. Are your arms getting heavy? Keep them outstretched as long as you can. Remember that Christ could not lower His arms because of the nails in His hands. Think of how He must have suffered.

Continue praying with prayers of gratitude or prayers for others. Do this without changing your position. Use the discomfort you are feeling to help you focus on what Christ did on the cross and how His suffering made it possible for you to have a relationship with God.

During this time, open your life to God; ask for His direction in your life. When your family prayer time is finished, ask your family members to bring their arms down to their sides.

Creative variation: Play a meaningful piece of Christian music as you cross-pray with your family.

Pray a Prayer Key Chain

"I like to pray. It's just that I sometimes forget to do it." James and his family had been

Could You Do This?

"Let's go, kids," Anna called to her grandchildren.

"Did Dad give you the money for us to use at the bookstore?" Joey asked.

"Yes," said Anna "I have it right here in my purse."

"What are we waiting for?" asked Matt. "Let's go."

On the way to the bookstore, Anna and her grandsons talked about books they had read together and ones that they wanted to get. The Christian bookstore they went to frequently had a large children's book section, and Anna made sure that her grandsons had a large stock of the books on hand at her house for them to read together.

"Do you think we will have enough money to get a new video?" asked Matt. He and his brother Joey both enjoyed the cartoon videos the store carried.

"I think you will have enough for one," said their grandmother. "Why don't you look at those while I look at some books for me, then we can look at books that we can read together."

When they walked into the store, the boys walked directly to the video section. Anna looked at the new titles that were out and picked up two that she was looking forward to reading. She then joined her grandsons.

"Did you find one you like?"

"Do we have enough money to buy two?" Joey asked.

"No," said Anna. "Your dad only gave me enough for you to buy one."

"But we really want two, Grandma," said Joey.

"I know, Joey, but you don't have enough money for two so we need to decide which one will you will buy."

"I think we should get this one," Matt held up his choice.

"But I want this one," said Joey in a small voice.

"Who got to choose the video on our last trip here?" asked their grandmother.

"I did," said Matt.

"Then I think it's probably Joey's turn to choose," she said.

"Okay," said Matt. "That one looks pretty good anyway."

"Great," said Anna. "Now let's go look at books."

talking about how important prayer is and how they would like to find more time to pray.

"I know," his mom said. "It seems like we are so busy with school and work and all the things it takes to run a family."

"It's like we know prayer is important, but we don't find the time to do it," said James's sister, Christie.

"I've tried to pray before I go to sleep, but I either get lost and forget who I'm praying for or I fall asleep before I finish." The other members of his family agreed with James.

"I saw a craft idea in a magazine," their mom said. "It showed how to make a key chain with beads on it. It could be used as a prayer reminder. Every time you hold your keys you can pray one prayer for each bead."

"Cool," said James. "Each bead could be a different color, and the color could be for a certain person or prayer request. I'd never forget who I was praying for that way."

"That would be great!" said Dad, "especially since I need a new keychain."

Fifty Nifty Idea #7

We have so many distractions in our daily lives. Wouldn't it be great to carry a reminder to pray, one that you could look at and know exactly who or what to pray for? The key chain you make in this activity will do that. Each bead on the key chain will be a reminder of someone or something that needs your prayers.

For this activity, you will need the following materials:

- ten-inch leather thong
- Key ring
- Colorful beads with holes large enough to thread the leather
- Small bowls to separate the bead colors (optional)

Have family members choose a bead for each person or prayer concern they want to add to their key chain. Ensure the number of beads doesn't exceed the length of the leather. Fold the leather in half so the cut ends meet. Pass the folded end of the leather through the key ring to form a loop. Then draw the cut ends through the loop forming a slip knot; pull tightly.

Family members can place the beads on their key rings by threading the beads onto each of the two cut ends of the leather. Allow enough leather on the end of each thong to tie a knot big enough so the beads won't slip off.

Compliment each other's key chains before you attach your keys. Ask everyone to tell who or what each bead represents.

To use your key ring as a prayer reminder, hold it in your hand. As you touch each bead, say a prayer for that person or situation. Try to pray through all the beads on your key chain at least once a day.

Your prayer might sound like this. "Lord, this yellow bead is for my grandma. She's not been feeling well lately. Please comfort her, and help her to feel better."

Prayer Bracelets

Claudia set the supplies she was carrying on the table. Interesting stuff like beads and strips of leather caught the eye of her daughter, Zoe.

"What's that, Mommy?" Zoe climbed on the chair beside her mom. "Whatcha' gonna make?"

"We're going to make special bracelets," said Claudia.

"Special bracelets? What's special about them, Mommy?"

"They are special because they can remind us to pray and what to pray for."

"I like to pray. How can they do that?" Zoe leaned in to the counter.

"Let's make them, and I'll show you," her mom answered.

Fifty Nifty Idea #8

This idea is similar to the key chain, but instead of carrying it in a pocket or purse, it can be worn. You will need the same materials used in the key chain activity; the length of leather depends on the wrist measurement of each family member.

Measure the wrist of each family member; add to this measurement 4 inches. Cut leather thongs in these lengths. Tie a knot two inches from one end of each thong.

Ask your family to carefully choose the beads they will add to their bracelet. Each bead will represent a prayer request and will remind them who and what they are praying for. These beads will be threaded onto the leather thongs.

Allow two inches at the end of the thong to tie a knot to hold the beads in place. Assist each family member in tying the bracelet onto their wrists.

As you did with the key chains, allow each member to tell who or what their beads represent. Take time to pray, using the bracelets as a guide.

Arrow Prayers

"OK, Garrett, it's your turn to pray," said his dad during their family prayer time. Everyone else had taken a turn to pray, and Garrett, as usual, was the last one.

After a long silence, Garrett whispered, "But, Dad, I don't like to pray."

"You don't like to talk to God?"

"No, I like to talk to God, in my head," he said with tears forming in his eyes. "I just don't like to pray out loud in front of other people."

"Oh, I see," his dad said reassuringly. "I can understand that. I used to feel really uncomfortable praying around other people, too."

"Really?" Garrett was amazed. "But you seem to like to pray now."

"It just comes from a lot of practice," his dad answered.

Garrett's sister Dawn spoke up and said, "My Sunday school teacher taught us a neat way to pray last week. It's called 'Arrow Prayers' because you shoot short, simple prayers to God."

"Cool. How do we do it?" asked Garrett.

"Let's say that you want Grandma to get better. You just say, 'Please heal Grandma'. Nothing fancy."

"I can do that!" said Garrett. "Let's pray."

Fifty Nifty Idea #9

Prayer doesn't have to be intimidating. Many times we think that to pray we must mimic the prayers we have heard from ministers at church or on television. This can put some people off, especially children, who think that they will never measure up to these prayer standards.

But, "Arrow Prayers" can be fun! These short, simple prayers challenge your family members to "shoot" prayers to God. Plus, "Arrow Prayers" don't have to be prayed at a specific time or even out loud. If you see a need or want to express thanks to God or just send up a word of praise, shoot an "Arrow Prayer!"

Ask your family members if there is a time during the day when they feel like praying but don't have the time, or they don't know the words to say. Most of them will probably say, "Yes!" "Arrow Prayers" can help your family achieve a more consistent prayer life and enjoy doing it.

Ask your family to think of something they would like to say to God. It could be a prayer request, a praise, or a thank you. Then tell them to put that prayer into one sentence such as, "Please help me with my test," "Thank you for my new job," or "Heal my grandpa, please."

Once your family members have thought of one or two "Arrow Prayers," you can shoot them up to God together. Encourage your family to pray these prayers throughout their day.

The A.C.T.S. Way to Pray

"OK, guys, let's get together for family prayer time," Lea's mom called.

Lea rolled her eyes as she got up from her chair to join her mom and sister at the kitchen table. "OK, I'm coming."

"What's that all about, Lea?" asked her mom. "I thought you liked to pray as a family."

"I like to be with you girls when we pray; it's just that sometimes praying can be so boring. I never can think of what to pray for," Lea said.

"Me, either," her sister Teri volunteered.

"Sounds like we need to change how we pray." Their mom opened her Bible and removed something from it. "I picked up a card at my women's Bible study the other day. It has an outline for a way to pray. We could try it and see if it gets us out of our rut."

Lea and Teri got comfortable on the couch while their mom brought some paper and a pen from the kitchen.

"OK, here's the way this works." She sat down on the couch with her daughters. "There are four letters: A, C, T and S."

"A.C.T.S.," Lea repeated. "That spells acts!"

"Right," said her mom. "And each letter is the first letter of a word. 'A' is for *adoration*. We'll start out our prayer by taking time to adore or love God. We wouldn't even have to pray this part, we could sing a song."

"I know some songs from Sunday school," said Teri.

"Next comes 'C.' That stands for *confession*. This is the part of the prayer where we ask God for forgiveness for anything we've done wrong."

"Next is 'T,' Mom," said Teri. "What does that stand for?"

" 'T' is for *thanksgiving*. We can show God we are grateful by saying 'thank you' for our blessings. And 'S' stands for a big word, *supplication*. Supplication is a fancy way to say 'ask.' This is when we ask God for things we, or people we know, need."

"You mean we could ask God to find us a new car?" Lea got excited.

"Exactly. Are we ready to get started?"

"Yes!"

"Great," said Mom. "I'll write the letters 'A-C-T-S' on the side of the paper vertically, and we can think of things to list that we want to pray about." Teri and Lea moved in closer to their mother, excited about the things they would be praying about.

Fifty Nifty Idea #10

How's your family's prayer life? Is it predictable or really exciting? Remember, we are talking to the God of the universe. If your prayer time is less than exciting, maybe it's time for a change. The A.C.T.S. way of praying can provide your family with a way to structure your prayer time. Instead of praying without direction, you will know exactly what part of your prayer you are on and what you are praying for—no more vague, repetitive prayers. Get ready to fire up your prayer life and make it a time your family looks forward to.

Grab a piece of paper and a pencil and gather your family. Say, "I have found something that will help our prayer time together. It's easy to do and it will help us know who and what we are praying for. This prayer strategy is based on the word 'acts.'" Each letter stands for a word that will help us fire up our prayer time."

Continue to explain to your family what each of the letters in the word "acts" represents. Write down the people or things that your family will want to pray for. Tell your family that "A" stands for the word *adoration*. What loving words would you like to tell God? Write these down on the sheet of paper by the letter "A."

The letter "C" stands for *confession*. What things are getting in the way of your relationship with God? Are there things you have done that you need to ask forgiveness for? Beside the letter "C," write down anything that you need to confess. Caution: there may be some items that family members need to confess to God but will feel uncomfortable talking about in front of the family. Allow them time to ask for some unspecified area of confession by just putting their names on the paper.

"T" is *thanksgiving*. What is your family thankful for? When you stop to think about it, this should be the longest section of your prayer. Look around at the things your family should be thankful for: your home, the family members you are sitting with, members of your extended family, your job, car, and friends. Write these items down and spend a joyous time in prayer saying, "Thank you, Lord!"

The last letter, "S," stands for the word *supplication*. It's not a word we hear much, and it means "to ask". What things would you like to ask God for today? Is it healing for a friend, help on a test or job responsibility, a better attitude? This is the place to ask God, so write it by the letter "S."

Pray together through the list you have written. Use the letters to guide your prayer. While you are praying, sit close to your family, holding hands if you like. At the end of the prayer, say "Amen" in unison.

Prayer Cruising

"Hurry up and finish your dinner, Shelly," her grandma said.

"Why, Grandma? You're always telling me to slow down when I eat," Shelly asked, shocked.

"Cuz we're goin' cruisin' tonight." Grandpa wiggled his eyebrows.

"Cruisin'.... what's that?" Shelly's younger sister, Darla, asked.

"That, my dear granddaughter, is when we get in the car and drive around town," Grandpa answered.

"But where are we going?" asked Shelly.

"When you go cruising," said Grandma, "you don't really go anywhere special. You just enjoy the ride."

"And this ride is special," Grandpa said, "because we're going to pray for the places we drive by."

"How come?" Darla asked.

"Because people need our prayers, and because God likes to hear from us," Grandma answered.

"But who will we pray for?" Shelly asked.

"Well, when we drive by your school we'll pray for your teachers and the principal. And when we drive by the park we'll pray for the friends you play with there," said Grandpa.

"And we could drive by Dr. Crocker's and pray for her and for our dentist, too!" said Darla.

"That's the spirit," said Grandpa. "Grab your coats and let's go cruisin'!"

Fifty Nifty Idea #11

When you stop and think about it, your family makes contact with a lot of people every day. There's the bank teller, the dentist, your child's teacher, the cashier at the grocery store, the list goes on and on. Did you ever stop to think that these people need our prayers? Maybe they have hidden needs, but you can pray that God will be with them. Or maybe you have been witnessing to someone at work or your child's school. This would be a great time to pray that God continues to work in their lives. Prayer Cruising offers your family a fun way to be together and a new opportunity to pray for people whose lives you touch daily.

Once your family has been buckled into their seats, explain to them that you will be driving around your neighborhood. Your objective is to pray for people you know and for businesses you frequent. For example, as you drive by your dentist, thank God for her and her employees and for how well they take care of your family. As you drive by your children's school, pray that the teachers will have patience as they teach your children. You may drive by your neighborhood fire or police department. Take time to thank God for these brave people who are willing to risk their lives to protect your family. If you have been looking for an opportunity to speak to someone about God, this would be a great time to pray for that opportunity to present itself.

If you find that your family is comfortable with this kind of prayer activity, make it a monthly event.

Popcorn Prayers

Darius put the bag of popcorn in the microwave and punched the "Start" button. After a minute he heard popping sounds. Soon they would have hot-buttered popcorn for their family game night.

"That reminds me of something I learned about prayer when I was a kid," said his uncle.

"What's that Uncle Joey?" Darius looked for a bowl.

"I remember learning a way to pray called 'Popcorn Prayers,'" Uncle Joey answered. "Your grandma would ask us to pick a topic like family, school, or thankfulness and we would say really short prayers about it."

The microwave beeped and Joey took out the popcorn bag. "So what would you say? If we picked thankfulness we would say stuff like, 'Thanks for my new bike,' 'Thanks for healing cousin Gary,' or 'Thank you for letting me get the teacher I wanted.'"

"I think I get it. You would 'pop' prayers to God!" Darius smiled. "I think I like that better than having to say or listen to a really long prayer."

Uncle Joey reached for the bowl of popcorn as Darius set it down. "They don't taste as good as real popcorn but I think God likes them, too. Let's play."

Fifty Nifty Idea #12

Like "Arrow Prayers," "Popcorn Prayers" are an easy, sincere way for your family members to pray. These prayers are short and directly to the point. Some can be prayer requests, others can be praises. They are whatever you feel led to talk to God about.

Though they may start out slow, once your family begins their popcorn prayers they will be like their namesake and come faster and faster as your family thinks of more things to talk to God about.

Put a bag of popcorn in the microwave or kernals in a pan on the stove and ask your family to listen to it while it pops. Ask them to notice that the popping starts out slowly but soon many kernels are popping at the same time. The same thing can happen with prayer. It may start out slowly, but as your family members feel more comfortable more and more prayers will be spoken.

Decide on a theme for this prayer time. Will you be praying for family, your church, friends, or your school or work? Once you have decided on a theme, begin your prayer with, "Dear Lord," then ask your family members to think of a short, one-sentence prayer that relates to the theme. If your theme is "our church," the prayers could be, "Bless our pastor," "Thank you for our youth group," or "Bless our mission trip."

When you have finished praying about a topic, move to another one and 'pop" up more popcorn prayers. End your prayer time by saying "Amen" as a group.

Ask your family members what they liked about praying, what made this easy or more difficult for them to pray, and whether or not they would like to pray this way again.

Inside-out Prayers

On the way home from church, Bianca was unusually quiet.

"What's wrong with you?" Her older brother Ray poked her.

"Nothing." Bianca scooted closer to the car door and out of Ray's reach.

"Yeah, honey, you've been quiet ever since we left church," her mom said. "What's up?"

"I don't know. I guess I was thinking about the part of the sermon when the pastor talked about turning our prayer concerns over to God and then not worrying about them. I try, but I still worry about things," Bianca said quietly.

"I have that problem, too," her mom agreed.

"Really?" Bianca sat forward in surprise.

"Yes, when I'm worried about something, I have a hard time giving it to God when I pray. It helps when I remember an activity we did once when I was a teenager," said her mom.

"What was that?" Ray was now interested in the conversation, too.

"Let me show you," said mom.

Fifty Nifty Idea #13

Praying is the easy part. The tough part is actually releasing those prayer concerns to God. God doesn't want us to worry; He will take care of it. This fun, inexpensive, hands-on activity provides a powerful visual lesson on how to turn over your cares to God.

For this prayer opportunity, you will need a lunch-sized paper sack and some pencils or markers. Place these items on a table or counter.

Gather your family and say, "Prayer time will be different today. We are going to turn our prayers inside out and give them to God."

Ask each of your family members to take a lunch sack and a pencil or marker. To do this activity, they will open the bag and use the pencil or marker to write their prayer requests inside the bag. Because the space is small, it will be easier to write one-word or short-phrase requests. Younger children can draw their requests. Tell them not to be concerned about their artistic ability; God will know what they are about. Then they can carefully turn the bag inside out and "turn" their prayers over to God.

Your family members then can tear their bags into small bits so that their prayers will remain private. They might want to keep the bag as a reminder of turning their prayers inside out and giving them to God.

Chapter Eight

Easy-to-Do Devotions Your Family Will Enjoy!

Then Joshua told the people: Years from now your children will ask you why these rocks are here. Tell them, "The LORD our God dried up the Jordan River so we could walk across. He did the same thing here for us that he did for our people at the Red Sea, because he wants everyone on earth to know how powerful he is. And he wants us to worship only him" (Jos 4:21-24).

Alphabet Devotions

Maddie rolled her eyes. It was devotion time again. She wondered if people got paid extra from making devotional material as boring as possible. She appreciated the fact her dad wanted them to learn more about the Bible, but did it have to be so boring?

"Great eye-rolling, Maddie." Her dad smiled. "I know the last few devotional books we tried have been, well, not very stimulating. But I think I may be on to something with this one."

"I think I've heard this before," Maddie said.

"No, really, and to prove that it's different, the only book we need is the Bible."

"OK," Maddie thought, "that is different."

"If you could study anything you wanted to in the Bible, what would it be?"

"Fear," Maddie answered.

"Fear it is," her dad agreed. "I'll just look up 'fear' in the index and pick out a passage."

Dad gave the Bible to Maddie for her to read the passage out loud.

"Now comes the fun part." He prepared to explain the Alphabet Devotion Process to her.

After following the steps, Maddie looked at her dad and said, "OK, OK, you're right. I like this one much better. In fact, I think I even understand what we were reading!"

"No more eye-rolling?"

"No more eye-rolling," laughed Maddie. "At least not about devotions."

Fifty Nifty Idea #14

This devotion is as easy as A-B-C-D. It is so simple you may be surprised at how much you actually learn about the Bible passage you are reading.

Start out your devotion time with prayer, asking God to bless it. Pick a verse or short passage from the Bible. You may want to use the index in the back of your Bible to look up verses on a specific topic such as love, hate, jealousy, fear, or faith. Read the passage aloud several times to become familiar with it. This would be a great opportunity for new readers to practice their skills. Use the following A-B-C-D questions to help you see what God is trying to teach your family through this passage.

A. What is the Bible passage About?
B. What is the Best part of the passage?
C. What part of the passage do you find most Confusing?
D. What does this passage call you to Do?

Jonah and the Bathtub Belly

"OK everybody, let's go into the bathroom," Rachel told her family.

"But I don't have to go to the bathroom, Mommy," said her son Alex.

"We're not going *to* the bathroom," said his big brother Tom, laughing. "We're going *in* the bathroom. Mom's up to something again."

After they all crowded into the bathroom, Rachel's husband Frank said, "OK, honey, now what?"

"I want you all to get into the bathtub."

"Uh, Mom," said Alex. "This is getting kind of weird."

"Just wait, Alex," she said. "It gets weirder."

Making sure everyone had gotten into the tub safely, she said, "OK, don't be scared. I'm going to turn out the lights and turn on the flashlight while I read you a story about a guy in the Bible named Jonah."

"Oh, I get it, honey . . . belly of the whale," Frank chuckled.

Could You Do This?

Anna was delighted that her grandsons were interested in learning more about Jesus. They really enjoyed their Sunday school class and always had questions for her when she saw them.

"What was Jesus like as a little boy?" Joey asked. He wondered if Jesus ever got into trouble like he did sometimes. "How can I be more like Jesus?" her older grandson Matt wanted to know. Anna knew it was time for her to give her grandsons more information about their faith, and this need brought Anna to her church.

"Hello, Anna," said Kate. "You're right on time." Kate was Pastor Craig's secretary. Anna really liked her church's new family minister. He was always available to talk with families about how to do faith activities at home.

"Hi, Kate," said Anna. "Thanks for working me in. I will only take a few minutes of his time."

Pastor Craig poked his head out of his office. "Good morning, Anna. Come on in."

Anna took a seat. "Pastor Craig, I don't want to take up too much of your time. It's just that I want to find some resources to help me teach my grandkids more about the Lord. They are starting to ask a lot of deeper questions, and I want them to learn that there are places for them to find answers."

"That's a great idea, Anna," he said. "And there are a lot of good resources out there for you to use with them. Now let me think, the boys are about . . ."

For the next twenty minutes, Pastor Craig and Anna looked at some books that he had, then they looked through some catalogs of other resources that she could order on the Internet or from her local Christian bookstore.

"Thanks, Pastor Craig," said Anna. "These will really liven up our conversations and maybe help me guide them to find some answers to their questions."

"I'm glad I could help. I may just have to call you if I have any questions," he laughed.

"Any time," said Anna. "Any time."

"We're not going to have any 'whale belly' smells here are we, Mom?" Tom was concerned.

'Yuck," said Alex.

Rachel carefully got into the tub with her family and began her story. "OK, you guys," she said. "Imagine what it would be like to be inside the belly of a whale. I'm going to turn out the flashlight and you'll see how dark it would be. Like Tom said, it would be really smelly and crowded with a lot of yucky things. Anyway, here's what the Bible has to say."

Rachel read her family the story of Jonah in the belly of the whale, and when she was finished they burst out of their "bathtub belly."

"That was great, Mom," said Alex.

"Yeah, Honey," said Frank. "I don't think I'll ever look at that story quite the same way again."

Fifty Nifty Idea #15

The Bible has some great stories in it. And what is more fun than listening to a great story? Acting it out! This activity will challenge your family's creativity to act out stories you have read in the Bible. By becoming involved with the story, your family will remember them more than by just reading them.

Choose a Bible story with a lot of action. You have many to choose from, such as Jonah and the whale, Noah's ark, Joshua and the battle of Jericho, and Daniel in the lion's den, to name a few.

Once you have chosen a story, read it several times and decide on the best place to act it out. The living room may be the best place for the battle of Jericho, using sofa cushions and pillows for walls; stuffed animals could make great "lions" for Daniel to face; and a bed filled with stuffed animals could be Noah's ark. Have fun with your story as you read; make animal noises, jump up and down, do whatever the story calls for. When you have finished your story, ask your family to describe their favorite part. Then ask them what they felt God was trying to teach the main character or characters in this story. Ask someone to share how they would feel if they were the main character in the story. Discuss how they would have behaved differently in the situation.

End your story time with prayer. Thank God for the Bible and for the lessons learned through this story. Pray for any prayer requests your family has.

Note: This will be the first acting opportunity for many family members. Keep the focus on what your family learns rather than focusing on their acting abilities. Have fun learning about the Bible together.

Your Family Devo Style

Kurt opened the devotion book he and his son, Michael, had been using the past week. They were trying to make it a daily habit to spend some time together in prayer and reading the Bible. For them, dinner had proved to be the easiest time for them to do this.

Kurt reached for the booklet after they had finished their meal. "Ready to do our devotions?"

"I guess," Michael shrugged.

"What's wrong, son?" asked Kurt. "I thought this devotion thing was going pretty well."

"I enjoy praying and stuff with you, Dad, but that book is really boring. Couldn't we do something else?" Michael asked.

"I'm open for suggestions," Kurt said.

"Well, couldn't we just read some Bible stories and talk about what God did?" asked Michael.

"Sounds like something we could try," said Kurt. "But we would still need to pray."

"That's OK," said Michael. "I don't mind praying anymore. I used to get embarrassed when I was little, but now I just talk to God."

"Exactly. Did you have a story you would like to start with tonight?"

"How about Noah? Man, that guy's neighbors must have thought he was nuts to build a boat and say that God told him to do it," Michael said.

"You're right, Michael. He must have really trusted God. Here's the story," he said as he opened to Genesis 6.

"Can you read first, Dad?" asked Michael.

"My pleasure," said his dad with a smile.

Fifty Nifty Idea #16

Every family is unique. The same is true for how you do your devotions. We have created our own way of doing devotions. We'll share our family style to jumpstart your creativity and develop your own style. Choose the devotion style that works for your family. Keep it simple. Make it fun.

We try to do devotions Monday through Friday. We usually have them during a mealtime. Sometimes we do our devo time while driving in the car. However, we were never able to establish the same time every day routine. We try to follow this format:

- Begin with a prayer.
- Share highs and lows from our day.
- Read a passage from the Bible.
- Ask questions like, "What is the author of this passage trying to say?", "What is most difficult to understand about this passage?", and "What encouraged you most about this passage?"
- Summarize passage.
- End with prayer.

That's how the Lynn family does it. What style will you choose?

Look It Up

It was a quiet Saturday afternoon, and amazingly the whole family was home. Marylee decided this would be a great time for her to do the Bible activity she had read about last week. "Hey everybody, come into the family room."

Doors opened and closed in different parts of the house.

"What's up, honey?" Max asked his wife. "Is something wrong?"

Marylee waited until her two sons joined them and then said, "Nothing's wrong. I just wanted to do a Bible activity I read about, and now seemed like a good time since everyone is home."

"Aw, Mom," Eric rolled his eyes. "I was on level three of my video game!"

"How about later?" Devin suggested. "I was just about to go for a run."

"And I was going to go to the store to get some ice cream so we could eat it while we watch the movie tonight," their dad said.

"Good try guys, but it all can wait till we're done. It's important that we do spiritual things together." Marylee gestured for them to take their seats.

"All we're going to do is go through the index in the back of the Bible and pick a topic that interests us."

"Then what?" Eric asked.

"Then we look up the verses on that topic and talk about them," Marylee said.

"Sounds pretty easy," Max said.

"I'll read some of the index listings," Marylee volunteered.

After she read all the listings through the letter "G," Devin suggested, "How about anger?"

"OK," she said. "Eric, can you write down these verses?" Marylee read the verses they would read on the topic of anger.

Each of them took a turn reading a verse or passage, then they talked about them.

"Wow," Devin said. "I didn't know the Bible had so much to say about anger."

"I can think of a few topics I'd like to look up the next time we do this," Max said.

"We could do another one now, couldn't we Mom?" asked Devin. "I could always run later."

"Yeah," his mom said. "I think we could do another one."

Fifty Nifty Idea #17

You won't have to purchase an expensive Bible study aid to do this activity. All you need is in the back of your Bible. There you will find a concordance, which is a listing of characters, concepts, and places talked about in God's Word. Beside the listings you will find the chapter and verse in the Bible.

Gather your family and explain that you have found a new way to study the Bible. This announcement may not be met with the enthusiasm you would like, but don't give up! Ask everyone to list topics currently of concern to them. You may want to start the list with words like: jealousy, joy, fear, etc. Pick one of the topics and look it up in the concordance. Then look up the verses printed beside the topic. Try to choose several verses in both the Old and New Testaments.

Take turns reading the verses. Ask your family questions, like "What did you learn about this topic that you did not know before?", "Was the information found in the Bible about the topic what you expected?", or "How will you use the information you found in the Bible?" Do at least three topics whenever you use this Bible study method.

Another way to do this Bible study is to sit down with your family members and learn about the topics in the order they are listed. You will learn something new—guaranteed!

Chunky-style Devos

"Come on in the family room," Becky called to her grandkids. "I have that new Bible I told you about. We can start our Bible reading together now."

"Oh boy," thought Conner. He really loved his grandma and appreciated how she took care of him since his mom died, but things like reading the Bible with her weren't exactly on his list of favorite things.

"OK, Grandma," he got off his bed and walked down the hall.

Becky smiled. "Don't worry, Conner," she said. "I think that you might like this way of studying the Bible. It's called a 'Chunky Bible Study.'"

"Chunky?" Conner asked. He shrugged, "OK, Grandma. Let's give it a try."

Becky turned to the Book of James and read the first few paragraphs. She then stopped and looked at Conner.

> ### Could You Do This?
>
> "Hi, Mom," said the voice on the phone. "It's Bonnie."
>
> "Hi, honey." Bonnie's mom, Mrs. Long, was glad to hear from her daughter, but concerned by the middle-of-the-day call. "Is everything okay?"
>
> "Everything is fine." Bonnie filled her mom in on some of the daily exploits of her grandkids.
>
> Her mom laughed. "Sounds like you've got your hands full."
>
> "Sad but true," Bonnie agreed. "Listen, I have an unusual request for you."
>
> "No, I'm not taking the kids until they are in college," said Mrs. Long.
>
> "Ha! What I need you to do is a little easier than that."
>
> "Okay, let's hear it."
>
> "I was wondering if you could pick some stories out of the Bible that you used to read to us when we were kids and read them into a tape recorder. Then you could send it to me, and I could play it for the kids at bedtime or in the car."
>
> "I could do that," said Mrs. Long. "In fact, I would be really happy to do that. The more stories they hear from the Bible the better."
>
> "My thoughts exactly," said Bonnie. "Thanks, Mom."

"Keep reading Grandma, I'm listening," said Conner, worried that his grandmother would think he wasn't.

"I'm done," she said.

"That's it?" he was surprised.

"Yes," she said. "Why don't you read it to me and then we will talk about what it says. Let's think of questions we can ask and how it makes us feel and then we'll talk about it."

"Hmm," thought Conner, "maybe this won't be so bad."

Fifty Nifty Idea #18

Just thinking about reading the Bible can be overwhelming unless you do it chunky style. This activity will be even more meaningful if you have a contemporary translation or paraphrase of the Bible that makes it easier to understand. Choose a book from the Bible you want to read with your kids. The Book of James would be a great place to start. If your children are younger, begin by just reading a few verses. Older kids can handle a paragraph easily, and you can take a whole chunk of the book if you have teens. No matter how much you read, try to stay on one subject.

Read the passage you have chosen. If your children are old enough to read, take turns reading. Let the words speak to you and then read them again. Allow your family to ask questions about the passage or express any feelings it evokes. Don't make editorial comments on their feelings. This is a time for your family to enjoy being together reading the Bible.

Don't look now, but you have just read the Bible with your family! And the best part is you spent time with your family in the best possible way—growing together in Christ!

A Proverb a Day

Sixteen-year-old Josh was sitting at his computer looking at a Christian online bookstore when he let out a big sigh.

"What was that for?" asked his dad.

"Huh?" Josh only half heard what his father had said.

"What's with the big sigh? You sound like you have a problem."

"Not a problem really," Josh said. "It's just that I was looking for Bible study material and most of it seems sort, I don't know, young for me. I really wanted to start studying my Bible more, but I can't seem to find anything that will get me started."

"I see your problem," his dad said. "I think I might have a solution for you. How about you and I read the Book of Proverbs together?"

"Proverbs?" Josh asked. "That doesn't seem like a book that I would want to spend a lot of time reading."

"Oh, I don't know. It talks about everything: money, power, greed, lust."

"Whoa!" Josh exclaimed. "Are you sure you want me to read this?"

"I think you can handle it," his father said. "That's the whole point of the Book of Proverbs, to give us wisdom to handle all sorts of situations."

"OK," Josh said. "You sold me. When do we start?"

"How about now?"

Fifty Nifty Idea #19

The Book of Proverbs isn't kid stuff; it handles some tough topics like power, greed, and sex. If you want to talk about these important issues with your teen and give them God's perspective on these issues, then this is the book for you. Ask your teen to read one chapter of Proverbs with you each day for one month (31 chapters fit nicely into a monthly schedule). Talk about how this advice from the Bible can be applied to your lives today.

God Titles

"Who's Jehovah?" nine-year-old Kendra asked her mom on the way home from church. "Pastor Davis kept talking about someone named Jehovah. Who is that?"

"Jehovah is one of the names of God," her mother Lisa said.

"You mean it's His last name, like Jefferson is ours?" Kendra was confused.

"Well, not really. It's more a title of God that describes what He is like. *Jehovah* is the German translation of His proper name, *Yahweh*. He has many other titles such as, *El Shaddai*, which means "God of the mountain." I know a few other titles are *El* (God), *Elohim* (Gods), *Adonai* (my Lord), and *Jehovah-Jireh* (Yahweh will see)."

Kendra thought for a minute. "So how many titles does God have?" she asked.

"I think it's something like 40," said Lisa.

"Forty?" Kendra exclaimed. "You're kidding me!"

"Well," her mom said, "I know one way to find out."

"Look them up in the Bible," Kendra said. "We could try to find all the titles of God. That could be fun."

"It could be a lot of fun," said Lisa. "And we might learn a lot, too," she thought.

Fifty Nifty Idea #20

Place the words "Titles of God" on the top of a sheet of paper. On the left side of the paper, write each new name for God that you find in your reading during the course of a year. Look up the name in a Bible dictionary to find out what it means in English. Write this definition on the right side of the paper directly across from the corresponding name.

Attach this sheet of paper to your refrigerator with a magnet. Each time you come across a new title for God, add it to the list. Refer to the list frequently in your family devotions to remind yourselves of who God really is.

Devo Shopping

"Wow." Michelle sat back in her computer chair.

"What's up, babe?" her husband Charlie asked.

"I didn't know there were so many devotional books to choose from," she said. "There must be 100 listed here."

Michelle and Charlie wanted to learn more about the Bible with their children, Grace and David. Even though the children were only preschool age, they felt it wasn't too early to help them develop a habit of studying the Bible. Michelle's early concerns about finding materials to cover with their children seemed to be unfounded.

"Are any of those for families with younger kids?" Charlie asked as he looked over her shoulder.

"That's why I am so amazed," she said. "These are *all* for families with younger kids."

"Some of these look like they would be a lot of fun to do with the kids," Charlie said.

"And there are DVDs of Bible stories and Christian music and story CDs for kids," said Michelle. "Let's order a few now, and this weekend we could take the kids to the Christian bookstore to pick out a few more that they like."

"Great," Charlie said. "You know, this looks like it's going to be a lot more fun than I thought it would be."

Fifty Nifty Idea #21

Your favorite Christian bookstore has all kinds of books that are age-graded to meet the needs of your family. Don't let family devotions get boring. Many stores have Web sites, too.

Now you know where to look, but what do you look for? Many books and Bibles are available. Consider the age or reading level of your child when making a selection. Toddlers enjoy picture books or simple stories read by a parent. Sturdy board books are easily held by small hands. Brightly-colored illustrations will grab your child's attention.

Encourage children who are old enough to read to look up verses you suggest and read them to you. This activity will help make their Bible more familiar.

Older children will enjoy reading autobiographies and biographies of heroes and heroines of the faith. Christian fiction books can help them learn through the power of a story.

Don't underestimate the power of music in your devotional life. Whether it's singing a song for worship, listening to music while you read or pray, or studying the words of a favorite old hymn, music offers a powerful way to draw closer to the Lord.

Go ahead, add a little variety to your devotions and look forward to spending some quality faith time together.

Chapter Nine

Creative Faith Conversations That Get Families Talking about Jesus!

Each generation will announce to the next your wonderful and powerful deeds
(Ps 145:4).

Mirror Faith Conversations

"Mom, there's something taped to the mirror in our bathroom," Emma said.

"Did you read it?" her mom asked.

"No, I was just surprised to see it," Emma said. "You really want me to read it?"

"Sure."

Emma read the note on the bathroom mirror. It said, "Why did God give us rules, like the Ten Commandments, to live by?"

"So," her mom said after a little while, "what's your answer to the question?"

"I think God gave us rules so we could live together without always fighting."

"Good answer," her mom said. "I think God also wants to protect us."

"Yeah, I can see that."

"Now it's your turn."

"What do you mean?"

"It's your turn to think up a question," her mom said.

"Can I tape it on your mirror?" Emma was already looking for a piece of paper.

"Sure."

Fifty Nifty Idea #22

When was the last time you talked to your kids about anything related to your faith in God? If you're like most families, you find it difficult. Mirror Faith Questions offer a fun, non-threatening way for family members to challenge each other with questions about faith.

Could You Do This?

"Lord help them," Anna said suddenly. She was driving her grandchildren to the playground.

"Did you say something, Grandma?" asked Matt. "I couldn't hear you very well."

"No, honey, I was talking to the Lord."

This was a normal occurrence when they were around their grandmother so neither Matt nor his brother Joey were particularly surprised that their grandma "talked" with the Lord. In fact, they would be very surprised if she didn't, since she seemed to have daily conversations with God just as if He were sitting in the car beside her or at the kitchen table.

"What did you say to Him, Grandma?" Joey was quite fascinated when his grandmother did this, then encouraged him to do the same.

"I said, 'Lord, help them,'" she answered.

"Who're them?" Joey wanted to know.

"There was a couple back there with a little baby. Their car had a flat tire, and I just prayed that the Lord would help them and that they could get on their way soon."

"Lord help them!" Joey prayed in a loud voice.

"Amen," said Anna.

Start by writing a question on a piece of paper. This should be a question about the Christian faith such as, "Why does the Bible say it's so hard for a rich man to go to heaven?"

Tape the question to a mirror that most of your family uses. Put it there early in the morning and ask your family members to think about the question throughout the day. Later in the day, at dinner, or before bedtime, share your answers to the question. Ask for a volunteer to write the next question and place it on the mirror.

Note to Parent: Don't worry if you don't know the answer to a question. Every parent has had to say, "I don't know" when talking about faith with a son, daughter, or grandchild.

Here are some sample questions to get you started.

- Name someone who has a faith you admire.
- Who is your favorite Bible character?
- Why does God let bad things happen?
- What is a fun memory you have of Sunday school?
- Why do you think so many people ignore God today?
- Who would you like to tell about Jesus?
- What do you think heaven will be like?
- What did you do today to make God smile?
- What would you like to do to help the poor?
- What time of day do you like to pray?
- Where do you like to pray the most?
- How is your family's love for each other like God's love for you?
- How does God want you to treat people who are mean to you?
- How do you sense God was with you during the past couple of days?
- What skill do you have that God could use?
- How have you said "yes" to God?
- What question would you like to ask God?
- How are the Ten Commandments helpful to you? To society?
- What do you think God looks like?
- What would you like God to change about our world? How can you help?

Faith Conversation Basket

"Dad, I think Mom left one of her baskets on the table. I want to set the table, so I'll just put it in the cupboard," Joe said.

"Mom didn't leave it there, Joe," his dad responded. "I put it there."

"OK." Joe was a little puzzled. "Should I still move it while we have dinner?"

"No, Joe, leave it there. I put some things in there that I want us to talk about while we eat dinner. If we leave the basket on the table, we'll remember to talk about them."

"What kind of things are in the basket?" Joe got the plates out to set the table.

"Articles and stories that will get us to talk about what we believe," his dad answered.

Fifty Nifty Idea #23

It doesn't take a Bible scholar to realize the more we talk about faith in the home, the more our children will have faith as adults. The home is the place where a child's faith is formed, with the church supplementing the family's efforts.

A Faith Conversation Basket will offer your family a variety of things to talk about. Family members can fill it with newspaper clippings, magazine articles, items downloaded from the Internet, or questions of their own.

For this activity you will need a medium-sized basket.

Put this basket in the middle of your kitchen or dining room table. Say to your family, "This is our Faith Conversation Basket. We can put all kinds of things in it for our family to discuss. Any time you read something on the Internet, in a newspaper, or in a magazine that you think would be good for our family's faith development, clip it out and put it in the basket."

Now your family can begin their search for items they would like to discuss. Once your basket has at least ten articles in it, you can begin your faith talks. Take time before your first discussion to pray together, asking God to use this activity to help your family grow in the faith and grow closer together.

Take turns drawing articles from the basket to talk about during mealtime. You can also talk while you are in the car together. Do this at least once a week, more if your family desires. Be sure to add new questions to the basket regularly.

Mealtime Faith Talk

It was dinner time at the Jenkins house. "Tonight we won't be just having a regular meal." Mrs. Jenkins sat down at the dinner table.

"What do you mean, Mom?" Ben eyed the food hungrily. It looked good to him, and it was making him even hungrier.

"I have hidden cards with questions on them that will help us talk about our faith in God," Mom answered.

"Where are they?" Ben's little brother Frank looked around the table.

"She said they were hidden." Ben rolled his eyes.

"Right you are, Ben," his dad said. "Your mom is pretty clever."

Could You Do This?

"Do you remember the ideas we heard on Sunday about how we can do more faith activities at home?" Liz glanced at Sam as she placed the bowl of salad on the table.

"Yeah, I remember." Sam took the dressing out of the fridge. "Why?"

"I'd like to try one tonight." Liz leaned against the counter. "We are all actually going to be home for dinner, and I thought this would be a great time to do it."

"So what are we going to try?" Sam gnawed on a piece of carrot.

"I thought we might start out with something easy. The pastor mentioned that we could take time together as a family to pray for our church's staff. What do you think?"

"Sounds good to me. Plus, they would probably appreciate it."

"Great! I'll call the kids."

Later, during their meal together, Liz brought up the idea of doing more faith activities together. "Pastor Gray had some good ideas for us to do at home, and I thought we could try one tonight."

"What do you want us to do?" asked Carla.

"Well, I thought we could say a prayer together for the people who work at the church," Liz said.

"And?" asked Louie.

"That's it," said their mom. "You look relieved. What did you think I was going to ask you to do?"

"I don't know," said Louie. "Maybe memorize a whole bunch of Bible verses."

"Nope!" His mom grinned. "I'm saving that for next week."

"Mom." Louie stretched the word into three syllables.

"Could I pray for my Sunday school teacher?" asked Carla. "She's not been feeling very well, and she has to have some tests done. I'd like to pray that she feels better."

"That's a great way to start, Carla," said her dad. "You go first."

"Can we start looking for them now?" Frank got up from his chair.

"Sure," said his mom. "The sooner we start looking, the sooner we can start talking!"

"And eating!" said Frank.

Soon the whole family was looking for cards. One was under the bowl of spaghetti. Another was under the salad bowl. Frank had one taped underneath his chair. In no time, they found all the cards.

As each family member sat down, they took one of the cards. As they ate together they discussed the questions.

"That was fun, Mom," said Ben. "Can we do it again?"

"Sure, Ben," his mom said. "I'll feed you again."

"Not that, Mom." Ben rolled his eyes. "The cards."

Fifty Nifty Idea #24

What do you talk about at mealtime? Maybe about your day or what your schedule looks like next week. It could be about how things went at school or at work. What if you could use this time to strengthen your family's faith and your relationship with each other? Mealtime Faith Talk offers your family a fun, creative way to discuss important issues of the faith together.

For this activity you will need to make a set of question cards. This is easy to do; all you need is some 3 X 5 cards, a marker, and some tape. Write a question from the following list on each card and hide them somewhere around your eating area. Possible places could be under someone's plate, taped to the bottom of their chair, under the table or a placemat, or another creative place.

Say to your family as they sit down to eat, "This is not a normal meal, this is a mystery meal. When I say 'Go,' I want you to look around your eating area for note cards. Once all the cards are found, we will read them together and discuss the faith questions they ask."

At the end of your meal, choose another family member to hide the cards the next time you pick a night for Mealtime Faith Talk.

These are some possible questions:

- How many hugs do you want to get from your family in a day?
- If you were given an extra hour each day, how would you spend it?
- What do you think Jesus looks like?
- Talk about a vacation your family would like to take.
- Name your favorite G-rated movie of all time.
- If God asked you to decorate heaven, what would it look like?
- If you could take Jesus on a family vacation, where would you want to take Him?
- Describe what changes you would make if you were president of the United States?
- Other than God, whom do you first want to see when you get to heaven?
- How much money do you think you need to be happy?
- What is the best thing God ever did for you?
- What room do you like best at church?
- What is one thing you own that you would never sell or give away? Why?
- What do you think is one thing God wants to do to bless you but you haven't asked Him to do yet?
- Describe your favorite toy.
- What is your favorite time of day or night?
- What do you do that makes God smile?
- What animal would have been the most fun to play with on Noah's ark? Why?
- Describe what you like most about your life now.
- Out of all the pictures of yourself, which embarrasses you the most?
- What do you think is the best thing to do when you make a mistake?
- What do you like most about coloring books?
- If you could have been the inventor of anything, what would you have wanted to invent?
- What is one question you have about your grandparents or great-grandparents?
- Talk about a popular movie that people are seeing this week.
- Talk about a time you felt really close to God.
- What is the best thing about becoming an adult? What is the worst?
- What does it look like when a person is cool?
- What would you buy if you had $100?
- Who has it easier—girls or boys?
- Name a board game you like to play together as a family.
- If you could go anywhere in the world for a week, where would you go?

Faith Talk Shuffle

"I'm glad you are going to be home tonight," Grandmother said.

"Did you have something that you want us to do?" Bill asked.

"Yeah, Grandmother," said Katie. "What's up?"

"Well, I want to do the Faith Talk Shuffle with you," Grandmother answered.

"The Faith Talk Shuffle?" asked Bill. "Sounds like a dance you would do at church."

"Do you play it like shuffleboard?" Katie wondered.

"Nope, it's actually a card game that will get us to talk about our faith in God."

"I like it when we talk together," said Katie.

"Me, too," said Bill. "Let's eat dinner and get shuffling!"

Fifty Nifty Idea #25

It sounds like a strange dance, but it's really a game that will help your family grow in their faith and have fun doing it. All you need is the set of cards with statements like those found below. Take turns shuffling the deck and talking about topics related to your faith. This game is created to be a fun way to get your family talking, so start shuffling and start growing together as a family and as Christians.

Say to your family, "We're going to play a new kind of card game. This game will help us learn about each other and about our faith. It's called the Faith Talk Shuffle."

Show them the deck of cards. Say, "I am going to shuffle these cards, and we will each pick one to talk about."

Shuffle the cards and let each family member pick one. If time is short or you want to have a long discussion about one topic, choose one out of the deck.

Cards you have used may be removed from the deck before the next shuffle or included to see what discussions might arise from them the next time you play.

To make the cards for the Faith Talk Shuffle, write each of the following (or some of your own) on a separate card the size of playing cards.

- Talk about a sermon you remember.
- Other than Jesus Christ, who is one of your heroes?
- What is your favorite Bible verse?
- Do you enjoy going to church?
- Say something about the Lord's Prayer.
- What's the most fun you've had helping others?
- Describe the funniest thing that has ever happened when you were at church.
- How could you introduce a friend to Jesus?
- What, in your opinion, is the best ministry in our church?
- If your faith were a color, what would it be?
- Why do you think bad things sometimes happen to good people? What about good things happening to bad people?
- Share an answered prayer.

- Say something about doubt.
- How do you do the "right" thing?
- How have you disappointed God? What has been God's response?
- How do you think God wants you to "lay up treasure in heaven?"
- Why do you think there is evil in the world?
- What do you know about your great-grandparents' faith?
- How are you a leader?
- Describe how the Bible has been helpful in your everyday life.
- Talk about what happens when a Christian disobeys God.
- What are some things besides God that people worship?
- Talk about something you could do to help the poor.
- Describe how new people are welcomed at our church.
- How do you want to be remembered?
- Describe what it is like when God forgives you.
- Where do you like to go to be alone? Where do you like to go to be alone with God?
- How can mistakes be helpful? Harmful?
- What spiritual gift did God give you to share with the church?
- What do you sense Jesus meant when He said, "Love your enemies"?
- Say something about the importance of worship with other Christians.
- How does God want us to think?
- How do you share what you have with others?
- Describe what God's love means to you.
- How would your life be different if you were not a Christian?
- When are you tempted the least?
- Talk about God's greatness.
- What does it mean to you to be a person of faith?
- Of all that you own, what would be the most difficult to give away?
- What's your favorite kind of weather?
- How does God help us make tough decisions?
- How could your faith in Christ help you achieve your goals?
- Talk about a time you felt close to God.
- What possessions do you need to give to the poor?
- How have you made your community a better place?
- Say something about money.
- What happens when you are not grateful to God?
- How is the Bible like a compass? How often do you use this compass?
- Tell a story about God's goodness in your life.

Faith Talk for Little Ones

"Honey, do you really think the baby can understand what you're saying?" Joseph asked his wife, Angela. The young mother was walking around the house pointing out different things and talking to her young daughter. "What are you talking about anyway?"

"I'm showing her all the different things around the house and telling her that God made them and that God loves her very much." Angela gave the baby to Joseph. "I figure it's never too soon to learn about that stuff."

"Yeah, I can see that. Even if she doesn't understand all the words she'll enjoy walking around with you hearing that God loves her." Joseph hugged his daughter.

Fifty Nifty Idea #26

Your baby enjoys being with you and hearing the sound of your voice. Use this enjoyable time together to start talking about faith with your child. It doesn't have to be anything complicated, just simple messages that God loves him or God created a beautiful world for her. These activities will set the stage for you to have more intense discussion about faith with your child in the future.

How do you talk to little ones about faith? Though it sounds like an impossible task, there are a lot of fun ways to do it. Here are a few for you to choose from.

God Made Me!

Take your child into the bathroom and carefully stand her in front of the mirror. Say to your child, "Let's play a game!"

Look into the mirror together and say, "Did you know that God made us?" Point to your nose and say, "God made my nose," then touch your child's nose and say, "God made your nose, too!" Then touch near your eye and say, "God made my eye." Your child can touch near her eye also and say, "God made your eye, too."

Continue pointing to various body parts as you say to your child that God made those too. When you are finished naming the body parts, point to yourself and say, "God made all of me!" Then point to your child and say, "And God made all of you, too!" Give each other a big hug and pray, "Thank you God for making us. Amen!"

Even When We Can't See

In a small child's mind, when he can't see something, it is gone. This activity will help reassure your child that even when he can't see you, you are still near.

Invite your child to play a game with you. Say, "Close your eyes while I hide, and when I call you, you can come and find me." Then go behind a large object or just around the corner, near enough so that if he becomes afraid you can go to him.

Make some kind of noise like a cat meowing or a dog barking. Ask him to listen to find you.

When your child finds you, hold him and say, "Even though you couldn't see me, I was right here. God is like that, too. Even though we can't see God, we know God is here." Play again if your child enjoys the game.

Pray with your child, "Dear God, I am glad to know that you are with me even though I cannot see you. Amen."

I Can Help!

Sit down with your child and say, "Even though you are little, there are a lot of things you can do to help take care of the world God made."

Walk outside with your child and look at a plant or some flowers. Say, "God made a beautiful world for us. You are big enough to help take care of God's world. One way to help is by watering these plants when they get dry."

Wash out a half-gallon or gallon plastic milk jug. Using a nail or knife point, carefully poke holes in the bottom of the container. Take the container and your child outside. Have him help you fill the container with water and then hold it over the plants to water them gently.

Say to your child, "You are helping take care of God's beautiful world."

Pray with your child, "Dear God, thank you for our beautiful world. Help me to take care of it. Amen"

Option: If your home does not have a yard, water a house plant or flower indoors.

Wonderful Colors

As you walk around your home with your child, say to him, "Look at all the beautiful colors God made."

As you hold your child, walk around your home and point out a variety of colors. Point to items such as pictures, leaves, flowers, fabrics, or paint. Name the colors for your child as you point to them and say, "God made that color, it's called (name the color). Isn't it beautiful? God must love us a lot to make such a beautiful world."

Help your child learn the names of colors by pointing to them and saying them together.

Pray with your child saying, "Thank you, God, for the beautiful colors that you made for us to enjoy. Amen."

God Keeps Me Safe

Hold your child as you walk through the different rooms of your home. Say, "When you are little, it is easy to get hurt. I love you and I want to keep you safe." Point out things in and outside of your home that help keep your child safe. These could include a baby gate, a fence, smoke detector, and outlet covers. Explain that for his safety, you pick up small objects that he could choke on and put away sharp objects that could hurt him."

Say to your child, "I do a lot of things to keep you safe because I love you. God loves you and wants you to be safe, too."

Say a prayer with your child, "Lord, help me to keep this child who I love safe. I know you love him, too, and I thank you for your protection. Amen."

Every Little Star

Go stargazing with your child on a clear night. Say to your child, "Look at all those stars. Our powerful God made them."

Pick out a star and sing to it the song, "Twinkle, Twinkle Little Star."

Twinkle, twinkle little star,
How I wonder what you are.
Up above the world so high,
Like a diamond in the sky.
Twinkle, twinkle little star,
How I wonder what you are.

When you finish singing, say to your child, "The same powerful God created you to be the special person that you are today."

Pray with your child, "Oh God, thank you for giving us the stars to remind us of your power and love."

Everywhere You Go

Even at a young age, your child can be aware that God is always present in her life. As you go throughout your day, whisper the reminder, "God is with us."

If you take a walk and see a beautiful flower, whisper, "God is with us." If you see the wind blow the leaves of the trees, enjoy a tasty snack, or hold each other while you are relaxing, say, "God is with us." If your child is fussy or upset, this is also a good time to remind her that God is still with her.

Pray with your child, "Dear Lord, thank you for being with us throughout our day. Amen."

I'm Scared

Have you ever thought your child may think that you are never afraid? After all, you are a grown-up and grown-ups don't get scared. Children need to know that it is normal to be afraid, and they can turn to God to help them with their fears.

While you are comforting your child after a scary situation, say, "I remember when I was afraid just like you are now." Relate to your child a story when you were afraid. It may have been during a thunderstorm or when you couldn't find your parents at church. Share with your child how you prayed or trusted God that you would be OK.

Allow your child to ask any questions he may have about your fears. It will be comforting for him to know he is not the only one who is ever afraid. Explain to your child it is OK to be afraid but God is there for him just like God was there for you when you were afraid.

Hold your child close and pray, "Dear God, thank you for being with us when we are afraid. Amen."

Super-Sized Love

Kids like to give and get hugs, and this activity allows them to do that. It also teaches them about God's love.

Kneel or sit on the floor beside your child. Ask your child to imagine what the biggest possible hug ever would be like, a real super-sized hug. Ask her to show you what this hug might be like.

When she has given you the super-sized hug say to her, "God would give you that kind of super-sized hug because He loves you so much."

Hug your child as you pray, "Thank you, God, for loving me as much as you do. Amen."

Kind Words, Please

Kids love to pretend. Pretending can become a fun way to teach your child about honoring God by using kind words.

Say to your child, "Did you know that God likes it when we use kind words? Two really important kind words that we use are 'please' and 'thank you.' Using kind words is important because it shows respect for God and for other people."

Pretend you are in different locations or situations such as at a store, in your home, or at a friend's or relative's house. Practice asking for something and saying "please," or getting something and saying "thank you."

Practice will help your child remember to use kind words. Continue to remind your child gently to use them. Forget to use kind words occasionally, and have your child "catch you." Teaching you will help her remember this important skill.

After pretending with your child, pray together, "Dear God, help me to remember to use kind words every day. Amen."

We Can Trust God

Your child trusts you to love and take care of him. The trust he has for you can be used to teach him about trusting God. Say to your child, "I have a game for us to play. Stand really stiff with your arms out to your sides. I will stand behind you and when I say, 'fall back,' you will fall straight back and I will catch you."

Your child may hesitate doing this and may need to look back to make sure you are there. But soon he will learn to trust that you will be there to catch him and he will fall back without hesitation. Say to your child, "You can trust me to catch you because I love you. You can trust in God because God loves you."

Pray with your child, "Dear Lord, I put my trust in you. Thank you for being near me when I need you. Amen."

Faith Conversation Placemats

"Whatcha doin', Mom?" Carl climbed up on the stool at the kitchen counter.

"I'm getting some supplies together for us to make some placemats," his mom answered.

"But we already have placemats on the table." Carl reached for an apple from the fruit bowl.

"Yes, and they are very pretty." Fran moved her supplies to the counter. "But our new ones are going to do more than just lay there."

"Really?" Carl pictured placemats doing anything else besides just laying there. "What are they going to do?"

"Something really special. They are going to help us talk to each other."

"But we talk all the time at dinner," said Carl.

"These new placemats will help us talk about important things, things we believe in."

"Do we get to color?" Carl spied the crayons his mother had placed on the counter.

"Yes," she said. "We get to color and write on these placemats."

"That makes them special already," said Carl.

"Why?" asked his mom.

"Because you've never let us write on any other placemats before," he laughed.

Fifty Nifty Idea #27

One of the best times of the day to find your family together is at mealtime. This makes it the perfect time for faith development. The conversation starters on these placemats can help your family grow in their faith and grow together as you discuss various topics. These placemats are so inexpensive and easy to make that you can make up a new set whenever you think up more faith questions.

Gather these items for the following activity:

- One 11" x 17" construction paper per placemat; use a variety of colors, if desired.
- Felt-tipped markers, crayons, or colored pencils.
- Clear adhesive paper to cover front and back after writing questions. You may also laminate the placemats.

Before presenting this activity to your family, think of a variety of faith questions to write on the placemats. These questions could include:

- What is your favorite worship song?
- Who is your favorite Bible hero?
- When is the best time for you to pray?
- What is a prayer that you know God answered?
- What is your favorite Bible story?
- Can you name the first five books of the New Testament?
- What question would you like to ask God?
- In what part of your home do you think the most about God?
- Where does your family pray together the most?
- Why would someone think you are a Christian?
- If you could do something today to help someone, what would it be?
- Who do you know that you would like to invite to church?
- What do you do that makes God happy?
- When or where do you feel close to God?

- What Christmas tradition do you have that you feel honors God?
- What do you like best about your church?
- Draw a picture or describe what you think heaven will be like.
- How do you show someone you love them?
- What do crosses remind you of?
- If you could invite Jesus to visit you, what would you do together?

Write each question on individual cards that you can give to your family to copy onto their placemat. Your family may also come up with more of their own questions.

Lay out your supplies on a flat surface. Say to your family, "We are going to make some new placemats. But these won't be ordinary placemats; these will help us grow as Christians and grow closer together as a family."

Use the markers to write down the faith questions in random locations on the placemats. Encourage your family to think of more questions and include those on the placemats you are making. Color or decorate the placemats as you like.

Peel off the backs of the adhesive paper and carefully lay it over the fronts and backs of the placemats and press to adhere. Or, have the placemats laminated.

Lay your placemats on your table. Choose a question or two to discuss before or after each meal.

Newspaper Faith Talk

As he sat down to dinner with his sister, Ann, and his dad, Joel asked, "Did you bring the newspaper to the table so we could look at the movie times? I really want to see that new science fiction movie that starts today."

"I brought the newspaper, Joel, but I want us to look at something else first." Dad handed him the newspaper.

"What's so interesting in the newspaper, Dad?" Ann asked.

"There is an article about some missionaries in the Middle East who are being imprisoned for talking about Jesus. I thought it might be interesting to talk about it."

"Wow! I didn't know that you could get thrown into prison for talking about Jesus. That's just wrong." Joel was visibly upset.

"What will happen to them?" asked Ann.

"I'm not sure, Ann," her dad answered. "Why don't we read the article and find out."

Fifty Nifty Idea #28

What do you talk about at dinner? If you are like most families, you talk about your day, the weather, the usual stuff. But what if you could spice up your mealtime or time spent in the car? Newspaper Faith Talk gives you the opportunity to do both and to enjoy watching your family grow in their faith as they learn more about their world.

This activity requires only an article from a newspaper, news magazine, or news story from the Internet. This article should lead you to a discussion of faith. It could be about persecuted Christians, cultural influence on young people, or something similar.

Bring this article with you to discuss at your next family meal or time together in the car.

Start the activity by reminding your family you are reading this article to them so you can discuss how the topic affects your faith or how you should respond to it because of your faith.

End your activity with a time of prayer for the people or concern addressed in the article.

Chapter Ten

Significant, Easy-to-Do Service Projects Your Family Can Do Together!

I also remember the genuine faith of your mother Eunice. Your grandmother Lois had the same sort of faith, and I am sure that you have it as well (2 Ti 1:5).

Tied Up with Love

Mrs. Canfield paid close attention to the directions given on the television.

"Even young children can help with this project," the woman on the TV said.

The project was a blanket. It required no sewing, just tying knots on the end of two large pieces of fleece fabric.

"That looks like it could be a lot of fun to do." She wrote down the directions. "The kids would really enjoy doing this." Her mind raced ahead to other things they could do with the blankets. Of course, the kids each would want one to cuddle up in this winter, and she wouldn't mind having one either.

"Hey Mom, we're home," called a voice from the kitchen.

After greeting the kids and her husband, she talked to them about the blankets.

"I want one of those," her son Jordan said.

"I think I would like one myself," her husband agreed.

"I think we can do that," she said. "But I was also thinking we could make some to give away to the crisis nursery or the homeless shelter. There must be a lot of folks who would enjoy receiving a warm blanket."

"Can we go look at the fabric now?" asked Sarah.

"I want purple," Liz, the youngest, added.

"Let's all go to the fabric store!"

Fifty Nifty Idea #29

A gift of a blanket brings more than just the blanket itself. It also brings the comfort of knowing someone cares. Many residents of children's shelters and nursing homes could use extra comfort, and your family can help. This is a craft project where everyone in the family can lend a hand. This is also a great activity to do with your extended family or with other families who would like to do a service project.

Before beginning your project, decide on the amount of money and time you are willing to donate. Each blanket will cost $5 to $10 to make, depending on the price of fleece. Many fabric stores have sales on fleece in the warmer months and after Christmas. This makes a great time to purchase fabric and get more blankets for less money.

Once you have decided how much you want to spend and the number of blankets you want to make, contact a local children's shelter or nursing home. Ask for information on the ages of the residents. If the blankets will be for children, ask for the number of boys and girls so you can make a blanket appropriate for each child. If cost prohibits you from making blankets for all the residents at this time, ask if you could make them for new children who come into the shelter or for any nursing home residents who have no family nearby.

For each blanket, you will need two one-yard lengths of fleece, 60 inches wide. Fleece comes in solid colors and in a wide variety of floral designs and prints. Shop for those colors and prints best suited to those who will receive the blankets. Wash the fabric before making the blankets.

Choose two complimentary pieces of fabric, usually a solid and a print. Cut off the selvage end of both pieces of fleece. For safety reasons, allow only adults or older children to cut the material.

On a flat surface, lay the complimentary pieces of fabric on top of each other, matching edges and sides. Begin cutting fringe along the edges of the fabric. These cuts should be 5 inches deep into the fabric and $1/2$ inch apart. Two or three pieces will need to be cut off at each end to form the corner when it is tied.

The next step is fun for all ages. To finish your blanket, all you need to know how to do is tie knots. Tie each top strip to its corresponding bottom strip. Tie each pair twice as if you were tying a loose knot. Continue around the entire blanket.

When you have finished your blankets, call the shelter or home you have chosen to set up a time when you can deliver them. If possible, use this time to visit with the residents.

Welcome Neighbor Box

As Jeremy walked to his apartment door, he noticed movers carrying furniture into the apartment across the hall.

"Finally, somebody has moved in there. I hope they have some kids." Jeremy felt like the apartment had been vacant forever.

As he walked into the kitchen, he noticed a pile of interesting things on the table.

"What's up, Mom?" Jeremy rummaged through the items on the table.

"See all this stuff?" His mom pointed to the things on the table. "It's not for you."

"OK," said Jeremy. "So who is it for?"

"We have new neighbors."

"I know. I saw the door open," said Jeremy, interrupting. "Do you think they have any kids?"

"As I was saying," his mom began again, "we have new neighbors, and I thought it would be nice for us to welcome them to the building by making them a basket of goodies. And yes, they have two boys."

"Cool," said Jeremy. "Hey, we're doing what we read about in the Bible ... loving other people like Jesus did."

"That's right! Now help me finish boxing this stuff."

Fifty Nifty Idea #30

Is a new family moving into your neighborhood? This would be a great opportunity to meet them and make them feel welcome. Moving can be a very stressful time, and a Welcome Neighbor Box is a way to ease the new family's stress and let them know that someone in their new neighborhood cares. It is also an opportunity for your family to express God's love.

For this activity, you will need a variety of materials.

- A clean box
- Gift wrapping paper
- Tape
- Flavored teas, coffee, or hot chocolate
- Pens and note pads
- A list of nearby points of interest such as theaters, restaurants, museums, parks, pools, playgrounds, malls, and grocery stores
- Emergency phone numbers
- Flower seeds
- Coupons

If the new family has young children, you can also include:

- Crayons or colored pencils
- Coloring books
- Cookies or crackers
- Bubbles

Cover the outside (and inside, if desired) of the box and tape securely. Before you fill the box, read John 13:34 to your family: *But I am giving you a new command. You must*

Could You Do This?

"Where are we going today?" Matt asked Anna. His dad had just dropped him off at her house on his way to work. He and his brother Joey could always expect some sort of adventure when they were at their grandmother's.

"Well," she said. "It's something that you've never done before."

"I've never jumped out of an airplane before," said Joey.

"Well, kiddo," said Anna, "I don't think you'll be doing that with me."

"So what are we going to do?" asked Matt.

"We're going to the church library. They have some really old Bibles I want you to see."

"Are they like ones you used when you were a kid?" Joey asked.

Anna smiled. "There are some that are like the ones I used when I was a kid, and there are some that are even older."

"Wow," said Matt. "They must be really old."

"I think they have one that dates all the way back to the Civil War."

"Where do they get the books?" Matt asked.

"People in the congregation have donated them."

"I don't think they will let us touch the really old stuff," said Joey. "Do you think they will have anything we can read?"

"I bet they have some Bible story books that we can check out and bring home," said Anna.

"Yeah," said Joey, "I like it when you read to us."

love each other, just as I have loved you. Take a few moments to pray for the new family to whom you will be giving the box.

Fill the box with several of the items listed above. Place larger items on the bottom and smaller ones on the top.

Deliver the box to your new neighbors. Use this time to introduce yourselves and to welcome them to your neighborhood.

Backpack Fill Up

"Oh, no." Jake looked at the display at the front of the store.

"What's wrong?" his big brother, Seth, asked.

"It's a 'Back to School' display. It can't be that time already. It seems like summer just started," he complained.

"It does seem like school is starting earlier every year," said Seth. "I should probably get some stuff while we are here. Do you know what you need yet?"

"Mom's got the list from my teacher." Jake looked over the display. He wouldn't admit it, but it was kind of fun to get new folders and pencils.

"What's that?" Jake pointed to a notice on the display.

"Let's see," said Seth. "It says that there are a lot of kids in our town who won't start school with the supplies they need because their families can't afford them. We can help by donating backpacks, paper, pencils, small calculators, and stuff like that."

"There was a boy in my class last year who always had to ask the teacher for paper to do his work," Jake remembered. "He always seemed really sad about that."

"Yeah, that would be embarrassing," said Seth. "Maybe we could help."

"How?" Jake asked.

"Let's talk to Mom and Dad tonight and see if we can donate some backpacks full of stuff."

"Cool! We can shop for them when we get our stuff," said Jake excitedly. "Mom will know where to take it."

"Good idea, kid," said Seth. "Let's get home and talk to them about it."

Fifty Nifty Idea #31

Back-to-school isn't normally the time of year when people feel the need to give. Unfortunately, it is a time when families could use a helping hand to buy school supplies their children need. Talk with your family about doing the following activity. Share the verse, *Children, you show love for others by truly helping them, and not merely by talking about it (1 Jo 3:18).*

How can you help? As a family, fill a backpack with school supplies. To do this activity, you will need the following items:

- New or gently-used backpack. If you purchase a used backpack, be sure to clean it with sanitizing wipes.
- School supplies such as paper, pens, pencils, crayons, markers, erasers, and cal-

culators. Perhaps you could purchase two of each item from your child's school supply list.

Contact your local school for information on how to donate your backpack. The school may have a list of students who could use help or you can find out the name of an agency that could deliver your donation. Some local television stations or retail stores have school supply drives to help those in need.

As a family, fill the backpack with school supplies you purchased. When it is filled, pray for the child who receives it, that he or she will have a great school year. Deliver the backpack to the school or agency. Although you may never know who received the backpack, you will know that you have showed love to others, just as 1 John 3:18 describes.

Care Bags

"Mom, stop!" Monica pointed out the window of the car. "There's someone over there!"

"OK, honey," her mom said. "Calm down."

"But Mom, we need to hurry. He really looks like he could use a Care Bag bad," Monica said.

The Lee family had been making Care Bags for the homeless people in their community. Instead of giving cash, each homeless person was given a bag of items that they could use such as granola bars, peanut butter crackers, an apple, lip balm, sunscreen, a juice box, and a note of encouragement.

"I think he really appreciated it," said Monica after she had handed the bag to the man on the corner. "He said he was hungry, so those snacks should really help."

"You're right, Monica." Her mom drove down the street to their home.

"I think we should pray for him, Mom."

"Good idea," her mom said. "You go ahead."

"Dear Lord, please keep the homeless man safe and help him to know that you love him. Amen."

Could You Do This?

"Who's that, Momma?" asked K.C. They were flipping through some old photo albums their grandmother had given to their mother, Bonnie.

Bonnie looked closely at the picture. "That is my cousin, Kenny. He was a little younger than me, but we always played together when his family visited."

"Who's the little girl?" Chris pointed to the girl standing beside Kenny.

"That was his sister, Lydia," said Bonnie quietly. "She died not long after this picture was taken."

"That's so sad," said Jenna. "What happened to her?"

Bonnie took a deep breath, remembering. "She drowned in a lake while they were on a picnic."

"I bet Aunt Joanie was really sad," said Chris.

"Yes," said Bonnie. "The whole family was for a long time."

"Maybe we should pray for Aunt Joanie's family," said K.C. "We could pray that they won't be so sad."

"Oh, brother," said Chris.

"I think it's a great idea, K.C.," said Bonnie. "I know if I was feeling sad, I would be happy to know that someone in my family cared enough to pray for me."

"Yeah," said Chris. "I guess that would be a good thing."

"I'll pray," said Jenna.

"Go ahead," said her mom.

"Dear Lord, thank you for our family. I pray that you keep them safe. And I pray that you will help Aunt Joanie not be so sad. Amen."

After they prayed for her cousin's family, Bonnie turned the page of the album.

K.C. peered over her shoulder. "Okay. Who can we pray for on this page?"

"I think the note we included will let him know someone cares about him, don't you mom?" Monica asked.

"Yeah, baby. I think he knows."

Fifty Nifty Idea #32

This activity not only shares God's love with the homeless in your community, but it can bring your family closer together while you do it.

For this activity, you will need the following:

- Large zipper-topped plastic storage bags
- Individually packaged nonperishable foods such as crackers or chips, gelatin or pudding cups with spoon, fruit such as apples or oranges, juice in pouches or boxes with straws attached, and granola bars
- A package of wet wipes or a napkin for easy cleanup
- A note wishing the person a good day or telling him God loves him. You can also write down a favorite verse

Before filling the bags, read Proverbs 14:31 with your family. This verse explains why it is important for us to do kind things for others. The verse says, *If you mistreat the poor, you insult your Creator; if you are kind to them, you show him respect.* Ask your family how giving someone a Care Bag is a way to show respect.

Pack the bags together, placing one of each item in each bag. Include a note that wishes them God's blessing for their day or that assures them of God's love. You may also choose a verse important to you and your family and write that on the note.

Bags can be delivered individually to homeless folks who are on the street asking for money, or they can be taken to a shelter where they will be given to those who need them.

After distributing the bags, talk with your family about the experience. Ask them what surprised them the most or how they felt they might have made a difference by doing this activity. Take time to pray for the individuals who received your bags.

Big Box Clean Out

Craig jumped in the car. "Hi, Mom! What's for dinner?" Food wasn't the only thing Craig thought about during the day, but it was after swim practice and he was hungry.

"Well, I thought that tonight we would have leftovers," said his mom, Mary.

"Leftovers?" This did not sound good.

"Yes, there are a lot of little things piling up in the refrigerator, and I thought we could just get them all out and have them for dinner. Sort of like a buffet," she said.

"But, Mom, some of that stuff is yucky." Craig remembered a seriously fuzzy bowl of green beans somewhere in the back of the fridge.

"Well," she said, "if it's yucky, we will throw it away, which is another reason I want to do this. I want to see how much food we are wasting. Too many people go hungry in this country for us to waste so much food."

Craig remembered the television show about hunger they watched the other night. When he first saw the program, he thought it was about a problem in another country. Turns out there are a lot of hungry people living in this country.

"OK," he said. "That doesn't sound so bad. But if it's furry, I'm not eating it!"

Fifty Nifty Idea #33

Can we end hunger? Not by ourselves, but we can limit the amount of food we waste in a world where people are dying of hunger.

For this activity, you will need a large trash bag and a sink full of soapy water. With the help of your family members, take everything out of your refrigerator. When you have finished emptying your refrigerator, wipe down the shelves, drawers, and door compartments. Throw away any questionable items, and return items that you can use to the refrigerator.

Use the following questions to evaluate the amount of food you waste and how this can be changed.

- How much food did you find that was spoiled (smelled bad, had mold on it, or just looked "funny")?
- From what food groups were most of the items wasted?
- Did you throw out a small, medium, or large amount of food?
- Is most of the food wasted leftovers or unopened food?
- How much packaging is used on the food you buy? More than food constitutes waste.

After your discussion, use these simple tips in your future food buying:

- Purchase more fresh food. These foods are more nutritious and waste fewer resources in packaging.
- Be more creative at using leftovers. Have a "buffet night" (sounds classier than "leftover night," but accomplishes the same goal). Lay out all the leftovers; add a salad or fruit, and you have a meal. Incorporate leftovers in other dishes such as omelets or soups, or use them as a side dish for another meal. Consider cooking smaller portions to reduce leftovers.
- Minimize food waste by covering and storing food properly.
- Don't feel guilty. These little changes can go a long way to reducing the food you waste in this hungry world.

Chapter Eleven

Faith-filled Family Walks You Won't Want to Miss Out On!

Do you remember the day you stood in the LORD 's presence at Mount Sinai? The LORD said, "Moses, bring the people of Israel here. I want to speak to them so they will obey me as long as they live, and so they will teach their children to obey me too"
(De 4:10).

Talk and Walk

"Come on everybody, grab your sweatshirts," Grandpa called.

"Where are we going?" asked his grandson, Jack.

"We're going on a walk."

"A walk? We've never gone on a walk before," his sister, Katie, said.

"Yeah, where are we going?" asked Jack.

"Well, not anywhere really."

"Then why go?" asked Katie.

"I thought it would be a fun way for us to talk to each other. You know, find out what kind of day we all had today. You'll have my undivided attention."

"Really? We can talk about anything?" Jack jumped up excitedly.

"Let's go." Katie pulled on her sweatshirt. "I have lots to talk about."

"I'm all ears," said their grandfather.

Fifty Nifty Idea #34

Do you know who are the most important people in the development of your child's faith and values? No, not teachers. Not friends. It's you! A great way to communicate your faith and values is by talking. Talking does not mean lecturing. Share your day with your child as he shares his. You can take a walk wherever you want, with no time limits. This is your time to enjoy your relationship with your child and to pass along your faith and values to her.

You don't need any preplanned agendas for this activity. Share about your day, something you watched together on television, a vacation memory, or a request for prayer. This is your opportunity to listen to your child. Listen as he shares his stories, concerns, and joys. Each of these topics opens the door to a teachable moment where you can share your faith. Share stories of faith from your youth, lessons you learned and questions you had. As your walk ends, take the opportunity to pray together for each other.

Take a Hike

"Look at that view," said Mr. Diller.

"I can't believe that we climbed so high." Nathan carefully looked over the side of the mountain.

"That's the nice thing about hiking. You enjoy the scenery so much you sometimes don't realize how far you've gone," Nathan's dad said.

"Can we do this again?" Nathan asked.

"Sure we can. I had fun too."

"I liked talking to you while we hiked, Dad. It doesn't seem like we get to talk much when we're at home."

"I know, we're all so busy," his dad replied.

"Could you teach me more about plants and rocks and stuff?" Nathan tossed a rock along the path.

"Yeah, I'd like that. It's always good to learn about the beautiful world that God created for us." Mr. Diller skipped a rock next to his son.

Fifty Nifty Idea #35

God's world is beautiful, but often our lives get so busy that we don't get a chance to enjoy it with our family. This activity will get your family out into nature where you can experience God's creation. This is your opportunity to talk with your family about how the animals and plants you see around them are praising God. Enjoy praising God with your family and with the creation all around you.

Choose a place for your family to take a hike. This could be a mountain, canyon, beach, forest, or desert. Don't overlook the park near your home.

You will need to wear appropriate clothes for the weather and sturdy closed-toed shoes. Apply sunscreen and insect repellent as needed. Before you leave, read Psalm 148 aloud. Ask your family to observe how the creatures and plants are praising God.

Point out any beautiful or interesting plants or animals you see on your hike. Because some plants like poison ivy can be toxic, be sure to caution your children to check with you before they touch anything. Some creatures can be dangerous when they are disturbed so it is best to look rather than touch. Hold the hands of younger children who may not yet have sure footing on uneven ground.

Before returning, stop and thank God for the beauty of creation by taking turns worshipping and thanking God for the creatures, plants, or other examples of our beautiful world.

A Walk Through Your Neighborhood

Tricia was helping her Aunt Betty unload groceries from her car. Her aunt's neighbor from across the street waved to her. Most of Betty's neighbors knew Tricia because she stayed at her aunt's house when her mom was working.

Tricia waved back. "Hey, I thought Mrs. West was in the hospital." She reached into the trunk for another bag of groceries.

"She got out last Tuesday." Her aunt closed the trunk of her car. "She seems to be doing a lot better."

"I'm glad," said Tricia. "I bet the prayers we said on our walk last week helped her."

Aunt Betty had decided that she needed more exercise and she wasn't going to do it alone, so now she and Tricia walked around the neighborhood together. Recently, they had started praying as they walked.

"I don't doubt it," said Aunt Betty.

"We should go again tonight," said Tricia. "A lot of other people still need our prayers."

"It's a date," said her aunt.

Fifty Nifty Idea #36

Ever give much thought to your neighborhood? Have you wondered about the people who live there or have businesses near where you live? How would your prayers for God's blessing affect your neighborhood? That's the goal of the following activity. It's not difficult; in fact, it will be enjoyable because you get to spend time outside getting exercise with the ones you love. While you are walking, you can stop and pray for friends, neighbors, your kids' school, the police, or fire station. This is a time to grow closer to your family as you lift up your neighbors and neighborhood in prayer.

Before going on this walk with your family, ask them if they know of any prayer needs in your neighborhood. Maybe someone's little brother is sick or a marriage is in trouble. Maybe an elderly neighbor has been ill or friends of your child are not getting along very well.

As you walk around your neighborhood, stop in front of the homes of the people you have talked about. Also take time to pray at your local school, police and/or fire department, and hospital or clinic. You can also pray for the safety of those who live in your neighborhood.

As you finish your walk, end your time of prayer by thanking God for this time your family had together. Thank Him for hearing your prayer.

Trash Pick-Up Walk

"What's all that stuff?" Monica asked her dad.

"It's for our walk today." Dad picked up plastic gloves and trash bags and put them in his backpack.

"We've never taken that stuff on our walks before," Monica observed.

"That's true, but this is a different kind of walk. This is a walk with a purpose."

"What's the purpose, Dad?" asked Monica. "I thought we took our walks to have fun."

"This will be fun, Monica, because we are together. We are going to the park to pick up any trash we see."

"Sounds kind of yucky, Dad. Why are we doing that?" asked Monica.

"God gave us a beautiful world, Monica," said her dad.

"I know; we always talk about that when we go on our walks," said Monica.

"Well, picking up trash is one way we can care for the world God created."

"OK," said Monica, "let's get started."

Fifty Nifty Idea #37

This walk has it all: prayer, family time, and a service project. God has given us a beautiful world and along with that gift comes the responsibility to take care of it. You can teach your family to be good stewards of God's gift and have fun doing it. It could be a day in the woods or at the beach, a walk around your neighborhood, or an afternoon picking up trash near your home. It's a chance to model for your kids our role as caretakers of God's world.

Before starting on your walk, give each family member age five and older a plastic trash bag. Older kids and adults can use the large, 33-gallon size, and younger kids can use small wastebasket-sized ones or plastic grocery bags. For safety, children under five should not be given their own plastic bags. They can hold on to the hand of a parent or older sibling and help them spot trash. For sanitary purposes, give each family member a pair of plastic gloves. If on your walk you encounter any broken glass or questionable items, take caution as you pick them up.

Be sure to dispose of your trash properly. Sort recyclables separately if your community offers this service.

Prayin' and Walkin'

"Look Mom, there's a water fountain. What kind of prayer can we pray that has to do with a water fountain?" Peter asked.

"I know, I know," his cousin, Lilly, said. "We could pray for God to wash away our sins! Get it, fountain ... water ... wash away our sins?"

Could You Do This?

"Hurry up!" Joey stood by the garage door, bouncing. "We're going to be late."

"We're fine, Joey," said his grandma. "We have plenty of time to get to church." Even so, in the next few minutes Anna, Joey, and his brother Matt all piled into the car and started on their way to church.

Anna grinned at him, then backed out onto the street. "Okay, Joey, tell us why you are in such a hurry."

"I don't want to miss the Bible story," said Joey. "Pastor Davis tells the best stories."

"I guess we'd better hurry then." She glanced at her older grandson. "What do you like about the worship service, Matt?"

Matt was quiet for a few minutes, and Anna became a bit concerned that maybe he couldn't think of anything that he really liked about going to worship with her.

He finally spoke. "I guess it would have to be the music. I like to close my eyes and imagine that God smiles while listening to us sing."

"What a great thought, Matt," said his grandmother.

"Do you think God smiles, Grandma?"

Smiling herself, Anna said, "Yes, Joey, I think God smiles. A lot."

"That's a good one, Lily," her aunt answered. "Let's look for something else that will make us think of something to pray about."

"There's a 'Wrong Way' sign on the corner," said Lilly excitedly. "We could pray that God shows us what *direction* to go."

"Or how about the 'Stop' sign? We could pray that God would give us an answer to a decision we have to make," Peter jumped in.

"Wow," said Lilly. "I didn't know that praying could be so much fun!"

"Yeah," said Joey. "You just got to know how to do it."

Fifty Nifty Idea #38

If you mention to your family that you would like to start praying together, what reaction do you usually get? It can range from bored yawns to looks of terror. How did prayer get such a bad reputation? Who knows, but with this activity your family will actually look forward to praying together. This creative way to pray offers a fun way for your family to spend time together and with God.

No matter where you are, at home or at a national park, you can take time to pray with your family. Once they pray this way, they will be asking to do it again and again.

Say to your family, "We are going to take a prayer walk. Any item you see can be used as the object of a prayer. If you see a tree, we can stand under it and thank God for the beautiful things He created in our world. If we see a store, we can stop outside and thank God for providing for all our needs. Just point to an object and we will find a way to use it in prayer."

It's that easy. Look for fountains, flowers, rivers, street signs, or power lines. Any object like these can be the basis for a prayer.

When you finish your prayer time, ask your family if they would like to pray this way again. If so, ask them what they enjoyed about this way of praying. To end your prayer time, hold hands and pray that you will continue to be this close to each other and to Jesus in the days ahead.

Cemetery Walk-Through

"What's up, Keith?" asked Artie. Since their dad left Keith, as the oldest, had tried to step in and take his place helping his mom raising his younger brothers, Artie and Lee.

"Mom wants us to get ready to go out," said Keith.

"Where to?" asked Lee, the youngest brother.

"This is going to sound weird," said Keith, "but she wants to take us to a cemetery."

"Who died?" asked Artie.

"Nobody died," said Keith. "She wants to go look at the gravestones."

"You're right," said Artie, "that's weird."

"Why a cemetery?" asked Lee.

"She said she wants to talk to us about death and how Christ gives us eternal life," Keith answered.

"Oh yeah, I know about that stuff," said Lee. "We learned about it at church."

"Well, it's time to learn some more about it," said Keith. "Go get your coat."

Fifty Nifty Idea #39

For this activity, you will only need a Bible. Explain to your family that you are taking them to a place where they can see what the Bible says about death and answer any questions they may have on the subject. Chances are when you tell your family that you are taking them to a cemetery, they will be concerned; cemeteries have the reputation of being scary places. But this location will provide a great opportunity to talk about Christ's gift of eternal life.

When you get to the cemetery, walk among the gravestones. Notice things like the dates people lived and died (some may be from a long time ago), unusual names, areas where a number of family members have been buried, or areas just for military graves. The graves of young children may distress your own children, so be prepared to answer any questions about why children sometimes die.

Your family may have questions about death. These may include what it means to die, if you have ever known anyone who died, or why the topic of death can make some people uncomfortable. Allow time for family members to talk about their feelings or concerns about death. Ask what was the most uncomfortable part of walking around a cemetery, or what they were thinking as they walked among the gravestones.

Find a shady spot and read 1 Thessalonians 4:13-18. Discuss the following questions:

- Why can Christians face death differently than people who don't believe in Christ?
- What might it be like to live forever in heaven with Jesus Christ?

End this time with your family by holding hands and saying a prayer, thanking God for the gift of eternal life through Jesus Christ. Thank Him that as Christians, we don't need to fear death.

Could You Do This?

Liz could tell that her husband had not enjoyed that morning's sermon. She had to admit that it was pretty boring and hard to follow.

"Did you follow *any* of that sermon this morning?" Sam asked his wife.

"Not really," she said. "My mind wandered through most of it."

"I cringe every time I see that he's going to be preaching," Sam said.

"What makes you cringe?" asked their son Louie.

Sam glanced over at his wife and saw her making cutting noises across her throat. That was the "universal wife signal" for "don't say anything more."

"Umm, nothing, son," said Sam. "I was talking to your mom."

"What?" Sam asked Liz later.

"I just don't think it's good to talk badly about the church staff in front of the kids," Liz said.

"I think they knew it was boring all by themselves, Liz. They're smart kids."

"I know." She sighed. "But my grandmother always said, 'If you can't say something nice about someone, don't say anything at all.' I just don't think it's a good example for the kids to hear us badmouth things about the service. They may end up not wanting to go at all."

"I guess you're right." Sam paused, then whispered, "But I still thought it was boring."

At the Mall Walk

Mr. Kendall took the calendar down from the wall and said, "It looks like tomorrow night is free for everyone. Let's do a family activity."

"Oh, boy." Carol rolled her eyes.

"I think you might like this one," her Dad persisted. "We're going to the mall."

"The mall, really?" her sister, Julie, said in disbelief. "You never want to go to the mall."

"There are a few things I need," said Mrs. Kendall.

"Well, we aren't going there to shop. We're going to go there for a walk," said Mr. Kendall. "It's a walk that will give us a chance to realize how blessed we are."

"This I've got to see," said Carol. "Count me in."

Fifty Nifty Idea #40

We go to the mall and come home with something we've bought. But do we ever come home with something of *real* value? This activity will not only give your family an enjoyable time together, it will also give you an opportunity to discuss with your family members what things have lasting value in your lives. Pick a night when you can be together and plan to see your local mall in a whole new perspective.

Before going on your trip, give each of your family members a piece of paper and a pen or pencil. Older children can help the younger family members.

Ask your family to make a list of things they would like to have if money were not an issue. Take these wish lists with you; you'll share them later.

After walking through a variety of stores together, sit down at the food court (or other seating area) and share your lists with each other. Ask your family to think about the following statement: "The best things in life aren't things." After a minute, ask if anyone would like to comment on the statement.

Read Matthew 6:24 to your family, *You cannot be the slave of two masters! You will like one more than the other or be more loyal to one than the other. You cannot serve both God and money.*

On the back of each person's list, ask them to make a new list. This one is of things in their lives that money cannot buy. This list might include things like the walk you just took with your family, dinner together, fun and games together, and holiday celebrations. After sharing these lists with your family members, say a prayer thanking God for those things on your list and buy a treat such as ice cream to enjoy together.

Chapter Twelve

Wacky Family Fun with a Touch of Faith!

This promise is for you and your children. It is for everyone our Lord God will choose, no matter where they live (Ac 2:39).

Progressive Fast Food Meal

"Uh, Mom," Grace said, "you only ordered one salad." This was a bit puzzling since four of them were supposed to be eating. It was the Romano family's Friday night out to dinner. This had become a family tradition ever since the kids had started school. It was a time for the family to reconnect and talk about their week. But it seemed like this Friday night meal would be a little different.

"I'll get the forks, honey." Grace's dad, Larry, picked four forks out of the container at the end of the counter and grabbed some napkins.

"OK, gang," said their mom, "here it is. Dig in."

"Does she realize there is only one salad?" Grace's younger brother, Paul, whispered.

"Who knows?" Grace took a bite of salad.

"I hope you are enjoying the first stop on our evening out," Mom said.

"Yeah, Gina." Larry winked at his wife. "This is pretty good."

"OK, you guys," said Grace. "What's going on?"

"You said it, kiddo," said Larry. "*Going* is the perfect word for tonight. We are going to a bunch of different restaurants to work our way through the meal."

"That's weird." Paul swallowed a mouthful of salad.

"What's next?" Grace wiped her mouth with her napkin.

"We were thinking about burgers and drinks at Burger Barn, and then maybe to Ralph's to share some of their fries," Mom answered.

"What's for dessert?" Paul was getting into the plan for the evening.

"Why don't we split a big banana split at Fred's? They make great sundaes."

"Grace, that sounds like a perfect ending to the meal." Her dad smiled.

Fifty Nifty Idea #41

We all have favorite fast food places. This activity gives your family the opportunity to visit all (or almost all) of them in one meal.

To begin this activity, sit down with your family and make a list of the fast food restaurants they enjoy visiting. Ask family members to be specific about what they like at a particular restaurant. For example, at one spot they may like the French fries, or at another they may like the burgers or pizza.

Once you have your list of restaurants, decide in what order you will visit them. To do this, you can use a meal's order of courses; for example, salad, entrée, side dishes, then dessert. Match the restaurants you have listed to the courses.

Load up the car and begin your adventure! At your first stop, order one large salad and a fork for each family member. At stop number two, order one hamburger, hot dog, or sandwich for each family member. If you choose pizza as your entrée, order a large for the whole family. At the next stop, you can share a large portion of a side dish such as French fries. Now you can go to a fourth restaurant for drinks or stop by the grocery store and buy a soda for each family member. (Order water with all the other food items to this point.) The last stop of the evening will be for your favorite dessert where you can share a whole pie or buy an ice cream cone for each family member.

"Why Be Normal?" Time

"I have something for you," Mrs. Simmons handed her daughter, Jessica, an envelope.

"What's the card for?" Jessica found an invitation to a birthday party.

"Uh, mom," Jessica said. "Why are you giving me a birthday invitation?"

"Oh, don't worry about that, Jess," said Mrs. Simmons. "Your brother got one for a bridal shower."

"Are you feeling OK?" Her mom was always coming up with surprising things, but Jessica wondered if she had really lost her marbles this time.

"I'm feeling all right, thanks for asking. But I'm definitely not feeling normal. Just read your invitation," Mrs. Simmons answered, mysteriously.

After staring at her mom for a moment, Jessica began reading the invitation. There was her name and a date and time for the party. In the space for the party's theme, it said, "Why Be Normal?"

"We're having a 'Why Be Normal?' party?" Jessica was confused.

"Exactly," said her mother.

"What is a 'Why Be Normal?' party, Mom?"

"Just read the invitation about what you are supposed to wear, and come find out," Mrs. Simmons said.

Fifty Nifty Idea #42

It's time for your family to take a vacation. No, not the kind for which you have to pack a suitcase and get out of town. This is a vacation from being normal! It's time for your family to get a little crazy and do some things you wouldn't normally do. In the daily rush, we often forget that families can have fun together. This extended activity gives your family a chance to see the world and each other a little differently.

What do you do at a "Why Be Normal?" party? Here are a few suggestions. With these and your own creativity, you're bound to have a totally abnormal time!

- Use any invitations you may have on hand to invite your family to this party, but normal invitations just won't work for this event. Write yours backwards so that they have to be read in a mirror. Get as creative as you want with colored paper, pens, and stickers.
- Decorate for your party! Use birthday banners, Easter bunnies, Christmas candles, red hearts, or anything else you have on hand, all at the same time!
- Since you aren't being normal for this party, don't dress normally. Why not dress backwards? Hats, shirts, pants, and jackets can be worn backwards. Be sure to mention this in the invitation so everyone knows how to dress for the theme of the party.
- Choose a different place than you normally eat for your party. Put a tablecloth on the floor or sit in a different spot. Start with dessert, of course! Desserts can be served upside down, frosting on the bottom of the cake, toppings on the bottom of the sundae—anything goes. Food coloring can turn normal food into fun food. Why eat plain white mashed potatoes when you can eat blue ones? If you make sandwiches, put the bread on the inside and two pieces of meat on the outside.
- Every party needs games. Consider some of the following games, with a twist!
- *Simon Says Don't!*—This game is played the opposite way you normally would play. When Simon says do something, don't. When Simon's name is not invoked, do what you are told. For example, if Simon says, "Touch your toes," you touch your toes. If Simon says, "Simon says touch your toes," no one should touch their toes
- *Old McDonald*—This mixed-up game provides lots of laughs. Sing the song, "Old McDonald" but use the wrong animal sounds for the animal mentioned. For example, if Old McDonald has a cow, the cow goes, "quack quack."
- *Tic-Tac-Toe*—Make Tic-Tac-Toe boxes and play in the usual way. But for this game, whoever doesn't get three in a row wins.

End your time together by asking your family what they enjoyed the most about this time. Also ask for any new ideas for the next "Why Be Normal?" party.

Family Fun Jar

"I'm so bored." Elliot flopped down on the couch.

"I know what you can do if you are bored." His dad was up to something.

"What?" asked Elliot, hopefully.

"Wash my car!"

Elliot rolled his eyes. "Come on, Dad, I'm not that bored."

"I didn't think so. But I do think you are right," said his dad. "We need something fun to do on afternoons like this one."

"We could watch a movie or play video games," Elliot suggested.

"Or you could take me to the mall." His sister Stacy walked into the room.

"I was thinking of something that we could do together as a family," said her dad.

Could You Do This?

"What's that?" Bonnie pointed to the magazine that her daughter Jenna held.

"I got it in Sunday school. It's a new Christian magazine for girls my age. It looks really cool. Not goofy like some of the ones that I've seen. There's stuff about clothes and friends and values. I'll read it when I get home."

"Yuck, girl stuff," said her brother, Chris. "Don't they have any good magazines for guys?"

"That's a good question," said his mom. "I'll call the church and ask."

The next day, Bonnie called the education office at her church. "My daughter brought home a magazine from her Sunday School class yesterday."

"Yes?" The woman on the other end of the phone sounded as if she were bracing herself for a complaint.

"Well, she really liked it, and I was wondering if there are any other magazines I can order for my family, especially the boys."

"Oh, yes! We recommend several magazines for the family. I can give you the names or you can go on the congregation's Web site and check them out. There are descriptions and samples of each one."

"Thanks," said Bonnie as she wrote down the Web address. "I'll do that."

After dinner, Bonnie asked her family to gather around the computer. "I checked out the magazines today. Here are all the ones that are by the same publisher as the one that Jenna brought home."

"Oh, cool," said K.C. "That one has an article about skateboarding."

"That one with the article about friends looks pretty good." Chris pointed to one of the boy's magazines.

"Why don't we do a trial subscription on those magazines and see if you like to read them." Bonnie silently thanked God that her kids were interested in reading anything but especially magazines that would bring them closer to God.

"I remember when I was little we would do things together," said Stacy.

"Maybe we can do them again," said their dad.

Fifty Nifty Idea #43

You won't hear, "There's nothing to do," when you have a Family Fun Jar handy. Use this activity to make the most of your family time together.

For this activity, you will need a coffee can, jar, or sack; construction paper in a variety of colors; markers; safety scissors; and glue or tape.

Decorate your Family Fun Jar using construction paper and markers. Glue or tape decorated paper to the container.

Next, give each family member a different colored sheet of construction paper. Cut each sheet into five slips of paper. Assist small children with this task as necessary.

Ask your family members to think up different activities they would like to do and write them on each sheet of paper. These provide your family with activity choices on long, boring afternoons. Fold the slips of paper in half, and place them in your container.

Each week draw a different slip of colored paper from the can. This will give everyone a chance to do his or her activity. When all the activities have been chosen, make a new set.

Newspaper Night

"Hey, Kevin, can you get the door for me?" called Dave, Kevin's dad.

"Sure, Dad," Kevin said, as he opened the door. "Uh, Dad, are you starting a paper route?"

"Ha, ha," Dave laughed, as he carried an armload of newspapers through the door. "Thanks. I've been saving these newspapers. I thought we could have some fun with them."

"With a newspaper, Dad?" Kevin was skeptical. "What could possibly be fun about the newspaper except the comics?"

"You'll see."

Fifty Nifty Idea #44

Who needs expensive toys and gadgets to have fun with their family? Chances are you will have everything you need for these newspaper-related activities around your home. Old newspaper, empty boxes, and waste baskets change from ordinary items to extraordinary sources of family fun. These newspaper-related games take little effort to provide a lot of fun and faith-sharing with your family.

For the following activities, you will need a stack of old newspapers, tape, large plastic trash bags, old blankets, rubber bands, empty boxes, and waste baskets. Read through the explanations of the following games, and pick one or more to include in your family fun time.

Newspaper Dress-up

Grab a supply of newspapers, tape, and your imagination. Choose a member of your family to be the first person to be "dressed up" by the remaining family members. Tell whoever you are going to dress up to stand still while you "dress" him in a newspaper costume. Decide the theme. Will you be dressing a soldier, a queen, a super hero, or a monster? Once you have decided, use the newspapers and tape to create the costume. If you have a large family, you can divide up into teams and admire the other costumes.

Where Did He Go?

For larger families, completely cover a child with newspaper as quickly as possible. To do this, divide into teams. Give each team a stack of newspapers and on the word "Go," each team will cover their designated child as quickly as possible. Smaller families can time how long it takes to cover a child and then try to beat their record. A fun variation is to have the kids hide the grown-ups!

Paper Route Roll

Give each member of your family small rubber bands and a stack of newspapers. Say to them, "The goal of this game is to make as many newspaper rolls as you possibly can in the time given. They should be rolled tightly enough for the rubber bands to fit easily around them."

Family members will have two minutes to roll their papers. The family member with the most rolls is the winner. Save these rolls to use for the game *Paper Route*.

Paper Route

For this activity, you will need a large room, preferably not carpeted, a blanket for each team; and the newspapers you rolled for *Paper Route Roll*. Place the empty boxes and waste paper baskets around the room. Vary the locations from easy to difficult. Be sure to move breakable items.

The next step is to divide your family into two teams. Distribute the newspapers equally between the two teams. Ask each team to choose a shooter. This person sits down in the middle of the blanket with the newspapers. The other members of the shooter's team then pull her around the room. While she is being pulled, her job is to throw as many newspapers as she can into the waste baskets and boxes. Only one team will make their paper route at one time. When the first team is finished, count up the number of papers that have hit their targets. Give the second team the same time limit. The team who hits the most targets wins.

"Snow" Ball Battle

This activity is just what it sounds like, a battle. But for this battle you will be using balls of newspaper instead of balls of snow. Divide your family members up into two teams.

Send the teams to opposite sides of a large room. Remove any breakable items from the playing area. Give each team an opportunity to build a barricade to hide behind. This could be made of sofa cushions or throw pillows along with chairs or other light-weight pieces of furniture.

Give each team a stack of newspapers and ask them to gather behind their barricade. Say to the teams, "When I say 'go,' you have one minute to make as many snowballs as you can from the newspaper."

Before the battle begins, caution family members to think safety. Snowballs should be packed lightly so they won't hurt when they hit someone. Ask players to avoid aiming for the heads of the other team members.

When both teams are ready, shout, "Begin the battle!" From behind their barricades the two teams will begin throwing their snowballs until they run out. Gather up the snowballs and begin again.

Price of a Meal Game Night

"Where are we going for dinner tonight?" asked 12-year-old Connor.

"I want pizza," said Hope, his 9-year-old sister.

"No, Chinese," said Connor.

"I could go for that," said his mom.

"I was thinking we could do something different tonight," Dad said.

"OK," said Mom, "how about Indian? You've always wanted to try that."

"No, I was thinking about not eating dinner tonight."

Mom thought for a minute and said, "Alright, if you want to stay home we could have pizza delivered."

"Yeah!" cheered Hope.

"Well, actually I wasn't thinking about ordering or going out for food," said Dad. "I thought ..."

"We aren't going to eat?" interrupted Connor, "I'll starve!"

"Don't worry, you won't starve," said Dad.

"I know they eat a lot, George, but we can't starve them," his wife said.

"Let me explain." Dad said. "I was thinking that instead of spending a lot of money on one meal, we could use that money to buy a game to play. We would still eat but we could afford to buy a fun game, too."

"So what do we eat?" asked Hope.

"I bet we have plenty of stuff in the fridge," said Dad. "We will be creative."

"This could be interesting," said Mom.

"We can talk about games while we eat," suggested Conner.

"Good idea," said his dad.

"That way," said Hope, "we can have even more fun while we're eating just figuring out what we want to buy. I like this!"

Fifty Nifty Idea #45

Going out to eat with your family can be a lot of fun. But this activity will make the fun last even longer by using the money you would have spent going out to dinner on a game to play over and over again with your family. Break out the hot dogs and the macaroni and cheese leftovers!

During your meal, discuss what type of games your family might want to purchase. Consider getting one that all ages will be able to play (with a little help, if needed).

Calculate the amount of money you would have normally spent going out to dinner. For most families, this will be at least $20. Go as a group to the nearest toy or department store and browse the game aisle.

After purchasing your game, if time allows, set it up at home. If no one in your family has played this game before, read through the directions several times out loud and play a practice game together. When everyone is comfortable with the rules, move on to play a real game together.

Mall Games

"What's going on?" Corey walked into the family room. "Are we going to play some games?"

Corey's dad nodded, holding a stack of games in his arms.

Could You Do This?

"What's wrong?" Anna asked Joey. Her grandson sat on the window seat, looking as if he were carrying the weight of the world on his shoulders. He looked at Anna with big eyes and quivering lips. "I can't pray!"

Anna sat beside her grandson and pulled him close to her. "Why can't you pray, sweetie?"

"I just don't how to say all the big words like you do. Even Matt sounds like a grown-up when he prays," Joey said about his big brother.

"You don't have to be a grown-up to pray, Joey," said Anna.

Joey's voice shook. "But I don't know the words to say!"

Anna thought for a moment. "You like to draw, right?" she asked.

Joey nodded.

"Well, maybe you could draw your prayer," said his grandma.

Joey was skeptical. "People don't pray in pictures, Grandma."

"God doesn't just hear, you know. God also sees. If you draw something that you are concerned enough to talk to God about, I think God will understand," she said as she pulled out the colored pencils and a sheet of paper.

"Okay," said Joey as he picked up a pencil and began to draw. Soon he had finished a picture of a woman. "That's my mom," he said quietly.

"What do you want God to know about her?" asked Anna.

"I want God to know that she doesn't feel very well, and I would like God to make her better."

"Joey?" said Anna.

"Yes?"

"You just prayed."

Joey paused, then smiled. "Amen."

"Yep," he said. "Go get your coat."

"But I thought you said that we were going to play games." Corey was confused.

"We are." His dad walked toward the door. "Come on, let's go."

Later, as they pulled into a parking place at the mall, Corey look at his dad and said, "Are you feeling OK, Dad? First you say we're going to play games, and now were at the mall with the games."

"We're going to do both, Corey. We're going to play games at the mall."

"But, Dad," said Corey, "what if somebody sees us?"

"My guess is that they will think we are having fun. Come on," said his dad. "Let's go,"

Fifty Nifty Idea #46

Maybe your family likes to play games together, but lately it's gotten a little boring. This activity will take the boring right out of it. No, you won't be playing different games; you'll just be playing them in a different place. Pull up a table at the food court and set up the game. You might get a few strange looks, and you may feel a bit uncomfortable at first, but soon the fun of the game will take over and you won't even notice. Those people who are staring might wish they could do something that fun with their families.

Choose one or two of your family's favorite games. Be sure all the pieces are in the box before you go to the mall.

When you arrive at the mall, choose a table at the food court area. Before playing, take time to thank God for the opportunity for your family to have fun together. Then start playing.

When you are finished, carefully pack up your games so that no pieces or cards are left behind.

Shopping Scavenger Hunt

It had been a long day, and the only thing Mrs. Fowler could think about was relaxing in her big overstuffed chair. Just as she sat down, her daughter Marti came into the room.

"Mom, can you take us to the mall?" Marti asked.

"Why, is there something you need?" Mrs. Fowler leaned back in her chair.

"Did someone say we were going to the mall?" Marti's younger brother Ben bounded into the room.

"Maybe. Mom's still deciding."

"I wasn't deciding," said Mrs. Fowler. "I was asking if you needed anything."

"Not really," said Marti, "but you never know. We might find something on sale or something really cute."

"Yeah, besides the mall's cool. All my friends hang out there," said Ben. "You guys could shop, and I can hang out at the arcade and see if my friends show up."

"Whatever happened to going shopping when you *needed* to?" Mrs. Fowler asked herself.

Fifty Nifty Idea #47

Mrs. Fowler has a point. It used to be that people only went to the store when they needed something. Now we go to stores at the mall to see friends, to walk around, to play games, or to see movies. This activity will take your family to the mall, but not to buy anything. Instead, your family will have a fun time together walking around and talking with each other about faith issues.

For the first part of the activity, you will need a list of items to locate on your Shopping Scavenger Hunt. You can use the sample list found below to help you make your own. Brainstorm with your family a list of 30 or so items for your hunt. Consider the stores in the mall as you make your list.

Work through the list as a family. If there are two parents and two or more kids, form teams with one adult as a leader. Although traditional scavenger hunts require you to gather items, your goal is to find as many items in the fastest time possible and mark them off.

Decide on a meeting place once the hunt is completed. The team with the most items checked off wins.

Sample Shoppin' Scavenger Hunt List

Place a check on the line before each item once you find it. Your goal is to find all the items on the list as fast as you can. The team with the most items checked will win.

_____ 1. Take a drink from the drinking fountain outside the watch store.

_____ 2. Find the aisle for the dolls at the toy store. Write the aisle number here:

_____

_____ 3. Write down the price of a birthday card at the greeting-card store:

_____

_____ 4. Locate a baseball cap at the hat store.

_____ 5. Name a product on sale. Record the name of the store and product:

_____

_____ 6. Write down the kind of cookies available at the candy store:

_____

_____ 7. Find the largest shoe at a shoe store. Write the size here: _____

_____ 8. Ride an elevator.

_____ 9. Watch 10 people ride up the escalator.

_____ 10. Count how many types of Bibles are at the bookstore.

_____ 11. Record the number of restaurants in the food court: _____

_____ 13. Get a drink from the water fountain by the elevator.

_____ 14. See what time it is on the clock in the food court.

_____ 15. Write down a brand name of a lawn mower at a department store:

_____

When your family has finished finding all the items on your list, treat them to ice cream. Discuss the following questions:

Questions for families with older children
- What does the size of the mall say about materialism in our country?
- How do you think God feels about materialism in the U.S.?
- What types of items did you see that people don't really need but that we buy anyway?

Questions for families with younger children
- What was the strangest thing you saw while you were on your hunt?
- Why do you think there are so many things available to buy?
- What one thing do you really need right now?

Pray together while you are at the mall that God will guide your decisions about buying "things."

Cross Talk Walk

"There's one," Bailey yelled.

"Where, where?" asked her cousin Becca.

"Right there." Bailey pointed down at the sidewalk.

There on the sidewalk were two intersecting lines that formed a cross.

"That's five we've seen," said Becca.

"You two are very observant," said their older cousin Kris. "You know what the cross stands for, right?" she asked.

"It's where Jesus died," said Bailey. "We read about it in the Bible."

"It's where Jesus died for our sins," said Becca.

"That's right, Becca," said Kris. "When we see one, it reminds us of how much God loves us."

"Look," said Bailey, running ahead, "there's another one."

Fifty Nifty Idea #48

You may not realize it, but you see reminders of the cross every day. It might be the telephone pole you pass on the way to work, the one on the church building near your office, or the intersecting lines on the sidewalk in front of your home. And each of these can be a reminder of how much God loves us and gave His Son to save us.

Ask your family to take a walk with you. Say to them that on your walk you will be looking for reminders of God's love for us. This statement may be met with some blank stares, but don't give up. Explain that you will be looking for crosses in any form as you walk. After your walk, talk about how seeing these "crosses" throughout the day can be a reminder of Christ's love.

Special Date with Mom or Dad

"Abigail, do you have any plans for next Friday night?" her father, Jim, asked.

"Hmm." Abigail consulted the social calendar in her brain. Seeing that Friday looked empty, she said, "Nope, why?"

"Well, I just thought that you and I might go out for a night on the town," said Jim.

"Really?" asked Abigail.

Jim could understand her surprise; this was not something they had ever done before. The whole thing started after he had read an article in a magazine that talked about how young women needed their father in their lives. It was important for girls to understand how they should act and be treated on a date, and having a dad take them out offered a way to practice this.

When Jim showed the article to his wife, she was all for it. "That's a great idea," she said. Connie and Jim had been praying for their daughters about dating and even prayed for the young men they would someday marry. Connie liked the idea that her girls would be learning from their father how they should be treated when they went on dates.

"One question," said Abigail.

"OK," said her dad.

"Why just me?"

"Well, because you are growing up really fast and if I don't go out with you now, boys will ask you and I won't get the chance," he said. "I want to spend some time together, just the two of us."

"Works for me," said Abigail. "Where are we going?"

"How about dinner and a movie," said Jim. "That used to be what your mom and I did when we went out."

"OK, Dad," said Abigail. "It's a date."

Fifty Nifty Idea #49

Moms and dads! Do you want to help your sons and daughters learn how to act and be treated when they start to date and have fun doing it at the same time? Ask your child to go out on a date with you! Arrange a time with her and plan an evening where she can go out and practice the social skills she will need when she begins dating. Not only will you have fun, but you also will have a lot of opportunities to talk about her questions and concerns on the subject of dating. You can share your values about appropriate dating behavior and pre-marital sex.

Family Time Capsule

After registering for a class at the university in her hometown, Denise walked through an area that had recently undergone new construction. The sidewalk was neatly paved with bricks except for one area that looked like a large manhole cover.

"That seems out of place." Denise stepped over a metal disk that had been set in cement.

"Time capsule buried by members of the class of 2005. Enclosed you will find memories of our time at this institution and of the world around us. To be opened on this date, June 2, 2055."

Of course she had heard of time capsules, but this was the first time Denise had ever seen one. She tried to imagine what the world would be like when the time capsule would be opened.

"I wonder what they will think of us." She tried to picture what the students might have put in the time capsule. Denise thought of her two daughters. "I wonder what kind of people they will be in 50 years. What will their memories be?" An idea began to take shape in her mind.

At dinner that night, Denise looked at her family. After explaining her experience at the university, she looked at her daughters and asked, "What would you think about making our own time capsule?"

"Mom," said Rachel, "that would be so cool. I can think of all kinds of things to put in it."

"We could put our pictures, and a copy of a current newspaper," suggested Julie.

"That's good," their mother said. "I also like to put things in that tell who we really are."

"Like what, Mom?" asked Rachel.

"Well," she said, "maybe one of your recital programs and one of Julie's drawings."

"You could put one of your favorite recipes." Julie laughed. She knew how much her mom loved to cook.

"That's perfect," Denise said. "Anything else?"

"How about some Bible verses?" asked Rachel. She recently had received a new Bible for her birthday and enjoyed the easy-to-read translation. She had already memorized several verses and had placed them on the refrigerator for the rest of the family to read.

"That's a great idea," said her mom. "It would let people know who we really are."

"Let's start now," said Julie.

Fifty Nifty Idea #50

Let's say you were given a chance to let people 50 years in the future know what your family was like. What would you want them to know? Deciding on what your family would put in a Family Time Capsule gives you the opportunity to talk about important things in your lives. Time capsules are intriguing, and they help us to focus on the future and what we would like people to know about us. While they are easy to make, they convey an important message.

Ask your family members to think about what items they would like to place in a time capsule if your family were to make one. Let each family member make a list. Help younger children who cannot write yet.

When you have finished making your individual lists, ask your family to reread their lists and circle the three most important items. Use these items to make one family list. Place this list on your refrigerator as a reminder of what is important to your family.

Some Possible Time Capsule Choices
- Parents' wedding pictures
- Items from your wallet

- Mirror
- Calendar from the past year
- TV guide
- Letter from a grandparent
- Bank statement
- Piece of sports equipment
- Dog collar
- Church bulletin
- School homework assignment
- Preschooler's drawing
- Address book
- School yearbook
- Pressed flowers
- Birth certificate
- Marriage license
- Book
- Diary/journal
- Diploma
- Baptismal certificate
- Report card
- Ticket stub from a trip
- Family Bible
- Lyrics from a favorite song
- Favorite poem
- Wedding ring
- Family heirloom
- Baby spoon
- Doll or stuffed animal
- Baby's blanket
- Magazine
- Favorite hat
- Christening or dedication outfit
- Newspaper
- Vacation pictures
- Special award
- Investment portfolio
- Favorite outfit
- Library card
- Christmas ornament
- Baby's first-year book/calendar
- Military uniform patch/medal
- Class ring

- Note from a friend
- Fraternity/sorority pin
- Easter basket
- Video store membership card
- Lock of child's hair
- Menu from a favorite restaurant
- Ticket from a sporting event
- Baseball card collection
- Party invitation
- Tithing envelope
- Sunday school attendance record
- School notebook
- Trophy
- Video game
- Family recipe
- Birthday/anniversary card
- Picture of a friend
- Movie video or DVD

Ask your family members if they would like to make a time capsule. If they choose to do so, collect several items from each person and place them in a large plastic bag or bucket. If you choose to include items such as a driver's license or anything you need for identity purposes, make a copy of these items to place in the time capsule. Be sure to mark out personal information. Additionally, avoid placing any items a child will miss, such as a favorite toy or stuffed animal.

Before placing items in the time capsule ask each family member to share why they chose their items, then decide on where to hide it and for how long. Place a piece of paper or tape on the bag identifying it as your time capsule and the date it was "buried." Choose hiding places such as a shelf in the garage or behind a piece of furniture.

HomeGrown Faith Resources Any Parent or Grandparent Can Use

Are you looking for activities to help you pass on the faith to your children and grandchildren? Are you looking for easy-to-use resources that make a difference? Are you looking for ideas that you can use no matter where you are in your own spiritual growth?

Visit **youthandfamilyinstitute.org** for all kinds of ideas and activities. Here is a sample of what you will find:

† Make Mealtime Family Time™ Kits
  Activities that engage your family in caring conversation, prayer, and family fun around the mealtime table

† Growing Up Christian Kits
  An assortment of Christian growth experiences the whole family can appreciate

† Stay-at-Home Family Night Kits
  Filled with fun-n-faith activities that encourage family time together at home

† Family Prayer Kits
  Creative strategies that will engage your family in praying together

† Can We Talk? Kits
  Get your family talking about the really important stuff

† Glove Compartment Grace Kits
  Fit-in-your-glove-compartment faith-growing activities for on the go families

† Faith-Filled Coupon Kits
  Easy-to-do devotions for families with kids of all ages

† Popular Bible Passage Kits
  Family fun with popular Bible passages from the Old and New Testaments

† Zinger Kits
  Real-life situations that help parents and grandparents talk with their kids about moral dilemmas from a biblical perspective

LaVergne, TN USA
02 February 2010
171813LV00001B/5/A